VIEW FROM A SHED

VIEW FROM A SHED

Michael Wale

CHIVERS

British Library Cataloguing in Publication Data available

This Large Print edition published by BBC Audiobooks Ltd, Bath, 2007.
Published by arrangement with Allison & Busby Ltd.

U.K. Hardcover ISBN 978 1 405 63920 0
U.K. Softcover ISBN 978 1 405 63921 7

Printed and bound in Great Britain by
Antony Rowe Ltd., Chippenham, Wiltshire

Brought up on a farm near West Hoathly, Sussex, MICHAEL WALE has always remained interested in agriculture and the countryside despite many years of living and working in London as a journalist and radio broadcaster. Four years ago he was involved in a fight to preserve allotment sites in west London, an experience that encouraged him to concentrate more on environmental issues in his journalistic work, moving away from his old speciality of sports-journalism. He has an eighteen-year-old daughter, is married and lives in Shepherd's Bush, west London, a ten-minute walk from his allotment.

Introduction

Sport has looked after me throughout my life. Even when I was asked to leave my prep school, after being revealed as the school's bookmaker, I was kept on for a term because I was the scrum half in an unbeaten First XV. It was sport that brought me my first allotment.

I had just returned to London after a spell in the countryside, where I rode racehorses for a hobby, and was persuaded to join the bowls section of Shepherd's Bush Cricket Club. The sport and venue suited me at the time, because I was working down the road at BBC-TV, presenting the nightly sports slot on the London and South East programme.

In the country I had a proper garden. Back in London I just had a tiny back garden. So I looked into the possibility of getting an allotment and, wheels within wheels, the then secretary of the Acton Gardening Association was also a leading member of the bowls club. When I gradually began to succeed at the competitive end of the game I was given an allotment as a guarantee I would stay with the club.

Later on, I gave up bowls, took up rowing as a cox and running 10k road races, but kept the allotment, and eventually ended up as secretary of the Association. The plot is a swift ten-minute walk from my house, and I go up there almost daily in the spring and summer, and at the weekends in the autumn and winter.

My interest in allotments grew as I researched their history. Our allotments in East Acton date from way back. Mrs Fuller, now nearly one hundred years old recalls watching from her plot as, in the distance, Italian prisoners of war worked under supervision on demolishing the local manor house during the First World War.

Poignantly, history has always been reflected by the land here. In the mid-1600s it had been left to the Worshipful Company of Goldsmiths for the good of the people of Acton by John Perryn, a local blacksmith born in Bromyard, Herefordshire, who had risen to be an alderman of the Goldsmiths company. Even today there is still a Bromyard Avenue, which runs alongside two of our sites linking the Uxbridge Road with the A40.

History, therefore, has always played a part. Now we have plot holders like General Safi who, as the Protector of the King of Afghanistan, was imprisoned, tortured, and finally escaped from his native country. There are any number of middle Europeans who have seen much but say little about it: a Kurd, who escaped Northern Iraq, as Saddam's soldiers set about ethnically cleansing the region; a Libyan left over from Gaddafi's dictatorship; in fact, altogether seventeen different nationalities at the last count.

The one thing they have found in common is peace and fulfilment in that very British piece of social history: the allotment. It also provides an opportunity to meet and talk with other people, because talk has always had precedence over gardening on allotments. It is only outdone by advice, which always causes us astonishment that television and radio should actually pay people to dispense what we all give away for free. They may be watched, listened to, or heard, but their advice is often held up to question, discussion and sheer derision.

*   *   *

Our own advice derives from various sources, orchestrated with wisdom by Joe Hughes, our chief plot representative, whose arduous job is to check that each of the hundred plots is kept in order and, if not, a warning letter must be issued by the committee. If no immediate action is taken to rectify the situation, then a plot can be reallocated.

Advice is like a baton handed from generation to generation. When I was first given a plot in the 1980s there was Norman, who used to hold Sunday morning advice sessions using a table beside his greenhouse. Norman was a great propagator. He could grow anything from a cutting, but he specialised in the growing of chrysanthemums and dahlias, and helped run the now defunct Acton Chrysanthemum and Dahlia Society, who organised a large local show annually.

I remember going there one year, when the local MP was Sir George Young the 'bicycling baronet', as he was known to the press. Sir George was a great friend of the allotment movement in Acton and Shepherd's Bush, and knew most of its members by name. We were both keen fans of the local football club Queens Park Rangers, and at one show he offered me his mobile phone to ring up and find out their result saying, 'I'm going to get the sack on Monday, the phone and the car will be taken away, so you might as well use it.' He was right. Mrs Thatcher duly sacked him the following Monday. But as long as he was our local MP he always looked after allotment interests and would have aided us in our fight for survival against the predatory Park Club.

The annual show only happened because of Norman, a natural organiser. Not only did he organise the show, but perhaps his *piÈce de résistance* was an annual dinner-dance at a local hotel for the allotment association, which he would also organise and appear in the cabaret, usually as a spoof version of a past musical hit.

Even his departure from the allotments seemed as if it had been choreographed. He

4

had not been well, and was due to return to hospital. Gathering a few cuttings he was growing in pots, he put them on a tray and walked slowly down the path to the gate. As he passed me he said, 'I'm off now, old boy. I don't think I'll be back this time.' Sadly, he was right.

Most of us on allotments have an obsession. One man would gather up spare pieces of land which people were not using and plant row after row of runner beans. My own obsession, I confess, is producing compost. If anyone wants to get rid of a compost bin I readily adopt it for my local council who sell them at half price to encourage home composting. As a result, at the latest count I now have five to feed with weeds, horse manure and our own kitchen waste. But my greatest secret is that they are watered with my own urine, which I store in old milk containers and bring almost daily to the plot and pour over the contents of one or other of the bins. Who needs Garotta, the overpriced product that is sold to activate compost-making, when you can use the real amber nectar? When I lived in Farnborough, Warwickshire, the village's best and oldest gardener, John King, always used to return from the pub at night and pee over his onions, which rewarded him with remarkable results.

Allotments produce eccentric human characters as readily as they do vegetables. In the past there was Ritchie who loved setting fire to things. The bigger the better. He would pour half a can of paraffin over anything, throw a lighted match towards it, and stand back and admire the sudden roar and spurt of flames skywards. This would be followed by an awful pall of black smoke. He would recommend the use of his flame thrower if you needed weeds, or overgrown grass, destroyed. Apart from his pyrotechnic skill, he appeared to do little as far as actual growing was concerned.

Even more eccentric was a person known simply as the Worm Woman; her belief was that the worms would do her digging, therefore she did not do any. She also brought to her plot lemonade bottles full of urine, but never used the contents. Just stored them until she had a lemonade bottle mountain. One day she announced that she no longer agreed to the over-orderly fashion in which the allotments were run and promptly left, leaving the lemonade bottle mountain behind.

But to return to Joe Hughes, who originates from County Mayo in Ireland and is a man brimming with philosophical wisdom. Only the other day he looked out from the warmth of his hut at the fine weather on a Sunday at noon and said knowingly, 'It's not a day to be indoors, I'm going down the Coningham.' He was referring to the Coningham Arms on the Uxbridge Road, which he visits every Sunday afternoon for a pint or two of Guinness, and to watch the Irish games of hurling or Gaelic football on satellite TV.

The best thing you can bring Joe, apart from a home-made Lincolnshire pork pie from the Saturday farmers' market in West Ealing, is an unwanted wooden pallet, which he proceeds studiously to take apart, removing nail after nail, and adding to his store of timber from which to create his next idea.

When I first joined the Association the committee used to meet every three months in a community shed at a nearby estate. No one really wanted to attend, and very few of the large committee did. Those who turned up could not wait to get away. When I took over as secretary I decreed things would be different. Now our committee meet almost every day over a cup of tea in Joe's shed. That is the way it should be. Allotments are living creatures and the things that affect them, like the weather, change almost daily. We're always aware of our huge battle just to exist, so we have to keep on top of things.

At any one time over tea there will be Joe, myself, our treasurer John Roberts, who came here from Barbados many years ago, and our new chairman Bill Geddes. Others will drop in and contribute, like Tony from the Vale site, and Michael from the Bromyard plots. By using this system we can react immediately to anything, anywhere, whereas in the old days it would have had to be tabled at the next meeting several weeks ahead thus making most decisions too late. There always remains the alternative of an Extraordinary General Meeting if there is anything the members really feel strongly that we are not addressing.

I have mentioned our neurosis about our mere existence. There is good reason for this. When I first had an allotment all our land was controlled by the Goldsmiths. At that time they were honourable and paternalistic landlords with a belief in their duty as major land and property owners to the local community. They even presented a silver spoon to the person who had done most for the Association every year at the Annual General Meeting. When planning permission was given for flats to be built on one of our allotment sites the Goldsmiths provided an alternative, and very good land for two more sites. There was not even an argument, as they saw it as their public duty.

Four years ago, however, there was a terrible turn of events. Together with their new estate agents the Goldsmiths decided to let half of their major twenty-five-acre site in East Acton to the newly created Park Club, part of the Hogarth Club in nearby wealthy Chiswick.

The first thing I knew about it was when a letter arrived from the Hogarth Club, giving all the plot holders of the Acton Gardening Association—nearly two hundred local people—three months' notice to quit. I felt quite sick. I now had to consider the position I had been placed in on behalf of my members, which the Park Club obviously thought were easy prey. After all we were just an oddly assorted bunch of allotment gardeners, with no power, and no public presence, who had always been protected by the Goldsmiths.

I remember within the first week of receiving the shocking notice walking around the bowling green of the Shepherd's Bush Cricket Club, also eventually to be evicted by the new health club, and talking with the captain of the bowls club, a working man, who said to me starkly, 'Money talks, Michael. They are richer than you are, and they will do what they want.' Although I'd heard these sentiments before, this was the catalyst that made me determined to fight our cause. Little did I think that the 'battle' would last more than three years as well as change the shape of my life, but the fact that my face and voice were well known did help.

The developers were totally within their rights. When I checked the lease, it said that only three months' notice was needed. It was a pretty poor document. Why hadn't I studied it more carefully before? Because in fact I had never seen it, and even if I had, I would have reflected the feelings of the old men who had signed it all those years ago. They trusted and believed in the decency of their landlords, the

9

Goldsmiths, and presumed their calm existence would continue for ever.

Through one of our members we heard about a local solicitor, John Vassello, who also had an allotment in South Ealing. I decided the first thing we needed to do was to negotiate a new lease, and get the draconian notice order removed. It was not easy. At least the Goldsmiths agreed to pay all our legal costs. Twelve months was the 'rule of thumb' notice under past allotment parliamentary legislation. But it applied only to allotments owned by local councils. If you were on privately owned land you had no real legal rights.

This caused our fall-out with the National Association of Allotment and Leisure Gardeners. I had pushed our membership forward, and our members had agreed to pay a personal levy so we could affiliate at a cost of £1 a head. One of the services offered was free legal advice. When it came to our battle the advice was negative: as we were on private land there was nothing they could do for us. As a result, we left the Association.

I heard on the grapevine that the Park Club also wanted to get rid of our next door neighbours, the Shepherd's Bush Cricket Club, who had played on their pretty tree-surrounded little ground for over one hundred years. We also heard that the cricket club were fighting their corner and coming to verbal blows with the opposition, which is just what the Park Club wanted, because they could then evict them if they did not agree to the terms offered them.

So John Vassello and I resolved a strategy where, when we were asked to go to the Hogarth Club, we would just sit and listen and bore everybody to death, which is precisely what we did. We met around the large boardroom table at the Hogarth Club's Chiswick headquarters. Colin White, head of the ruling family, chaired the meeting. Also present was an estate agent from Knight Rutley, the Hogarth's resident lawyer, and Patrick White, the younger son. At least we came away with the three-month notice withdrawn, and a promise to draw up a new twelve-month lease, with notice to be given, if any, by the 27th of September annually. We agreed to give up our allotment site, with at least fifty beautifully kept plots, adjoining the about-to-be-built Park Club, and ended the day with no rancour, fixing a date for a meeting next month. The reason we gave our plots up was that they surrounded the planned new club building, and would obviously be in the club's way, because they wanted to build tennis courts and an outdoor swimming pool. Also, by giving up this block of plots the Park Club promised us that the rest of our sites would remain untouched.

Meanwhile, we held an Extraordinary

General Meeting at the Acton Vale Social Club. We also launched a press offensive backed by the local *Ealing and Acton Gazette*, alerted our local councillors, and contacted our MP Clive Soley. The original three-month notice had had a devastating effect upon our membership, many of whom felt they did not want to work their plots anymore. It certainly affected me that way. But we had to warn our members that this was probably a tactic of our opponents who wanted the land to fall into disuse. A scorched-earth policy.

Although the new lease was being prepared, Colin White kept the pressure on by making a series of requests which we felt unable to comply with: the names and addresses of each of our members; the need for our shop to be closed; an instruction that, in future, a female employee of the Hogarth Club would be responsible for managing the allotments on behalf of the new landlords. We kept our nerve, but at times I felt depressed by the whole business. I was being asked questions by the members that I was unable to answer, because of lack of information. Other members wanted a more bullish, direct-action approach in our tactical battle, while John Vassello and I believed that our softly softly plan would, at the very least, guarantee our future.

The breakthrough came after a year following a telephone conversation with

Patrick White, who seemed the only reasonable person in the enemy camp. It was at the height of the delicate monthly meetings when I suggested that we meet alone in a café in Chiswick. It turned out that we had a mutual friend, the writer Gordon Williams, whose best-known work was his novel, *The Siege of Trencherman's Farm*, later made into a violent film called *Straw Dogs*, directed by Sam Peckinpah.

Patrick turned out to be a very interesting and talented person. He had studied English literature at Cambridge, studied business and worked in America and loved cricket. He realised that the bombastic approach of his father had not endeared him to local people, whereas we had gained the publicity advantage, culminating in the *Ealing and Acton Gazette* writing a leader in our favour.

First of all, Patrick said that he couldn't really believe we were sitting down together, and alone. I reminded him that at the height of the IRA atrocities I was sure that agents from the British government met with them secretly. It had always happened throughout history. So why not solve our own much simpler problems this way. Obviously if my members had known at the time they would not have liked it, and neither would the Park Club.

Both Patrick and I were taking a risk, but it worked. I told him what I really wanted, and

13

that was a new lease, a guarantee of our future, and that the land left that was being used for allotments would always be used for that purpose. He agreed to push the plan through as long as we left another site. If we left this site, next door to the site we had already vacated and within the close boundaries of the newly built upmarket health club, then we could have the rest of the sites at a peppercorn rent (in other words for nothing), work out a guarantee of longevity plus install new water systems and fencing at the club's expense.

After our meeting there was a final blow, with a letter of apology from Patrick saying that he had just been told that the Park Club wanted to build a road through the middle of our Chestnuts site leading to a car park. As a result, we accepted twelve months' notice on the four plots that would be affected, but won a small victory by being given land for new plots on the next door Perryn site. At last we had actually gained some land. Yet, it could never be compared with what we had lost. Still, because there had been a hard-surface tennis court a few feet under the new land, Patrick agreed to truck several loads of topsoil from Kent to make the ground fit for growing.

The climax came at a public meeting of the London Borough of Ealing's Planning Committee. A Section 106 agreement had been drawn up, this being the Planning Gain invention, which usually leads to the big beating the small. In return for planning permission the developer, often a supermarket, has to offer something in exchange, such as low-cost housing, or a new road. It is, in my opinion, a very unreliable piece of legislation, which was not made in the public interest and is open to all sorts of chicanery. However, on this occasion we got a Section 106 in reverse. In return for agreeing to the new road, we would get the seven new allotments on some waste land behind the Perryn site, the new water system, new security fencing and £50,000 would be paid for the use of allotments in East Acton, but not to us. A further sum of money would be spent on the development of Oak Way on the Vale estate next to our Vale site. It would also be guaranteed that all the remaining allotment land under our cultivation would be protected and only be used for allotments for the next ninety years.

As I came out of Ealing Town Hall after the meeting the Park Club group of lawyers and grandees were already on the steps. I turned to Colin White: 'I learned a lot from you, Colin,' to which he replied, 'And I've learned a lot from you.' Our campaign had cost them a fair amount of money and lost them the public relations war.

However, the agreement has yet to be signed. Whenever I enquire, each side blames the other for the delay. I have even spoken on the phone to Jimmy Umriga, who is handling the contract for Ealing's legal department. Two years after it should have been signed I wrote to London's Mayor Ken Livingstone, who allegedly backs green open space in the capital. In January a reply arrived from City Hall. It said:

Dear Michael Wale.

Section 106 on allotment land in East Acton.

Thank you for your letter dated 16 November 2004 regarding the delay in the signing of a Section 106 agreement between Ealing Borough Council and the Park Club over allotment land in East Acton.

While I sympathise with your frustration at the length of time that the Section 106 has taken, this is a matter for the council and the Park Club to resolve. Unfortunately the Mayor does not have any remit to take forward complaints against the behaviour of councils and you should contact the council to make a complaint using their complaints procedure.

It is signed by someone on behalf of John O' Neil, Senior Planner.

Interestingly, on the 1st of January, 2005,

the Freedom of Information Act came into being, stating that everyone has the right to apply for specific information from all sorts of authorities including local councils. So this is the course I will now take. I have also been advised to consult the Local Government Ombudsman.

I have also made contact with our local councillor Paul Woodgate, who has been involved all along, to bring this whole farce to a conclusion. Ironically, his emailed reply says that he might have to use the Freedom of Information Act. Patrick White rang me almost a year after the decision, off the record, to say they would not be taking up the four plots needed for the road and we could have them back. The road and car park plan were no more. It was said locally that the school opposite us had strongly protested.

Running a modern allotment is very different from the past, when all the officials had to worry about was the width of the paths and whether the plots were properly maintained. They were very gentlemanly days. The majority of plot holders were men. There were few women who had plots and usually, if they did, they shared a plot with their husband. All that has changed radically in the last few years.

Winter/Spring

This is the brave beginning of the growing year, when optimism rules and you believe everything the seed catalogues have told you all winter, even after three days of solid rain has washed away your first planting of carrots.

Seed catalogues have a strange effect on me. Reading the descriptions in car or property catalogues, I am highly cynical and hardly believe a word I read. But I believe everything I read in a seed catalogue: whether this is because they're usually read in mid-winter when all is dark and cold and depressing, and you are searching for dreams, or the confirmation of dreams, I am not sure. It is another world with compelling colour photographs as well as colourful words to accompany them. I always know my order will be more than I am able to plant, and yet the process is repeated every year.

But this moment in the allotment year is like the start of the football season. Everyone, everywhere, is going to be a winner!

One of the great innovations of our new season is the arrival of the polytunnel to provide ready-grown plants for the members. It is one of those innovations that make the not so distant past seem years ago. It is entirely self-heated by its special plastic wrapping. It filters whatever weak sunshine there is, and multiplies it. What a wonderful invention.

Its installation is yet another example of the building skills of Joe Hughes, who planned its construction, thus keeping the price to a minimum. If we had bought the whole structure from the helpful Lancashire firm of First Tunnels, it would have cost several hundred pounds. To make the curved supports, Joe used the piping that was surplus to what he needed for the huge new water scheme he was planning. From the numerous wooden pallets we all collected and brought to the site, he had built the benches for the seed trays on each side of the polytunnel.

Joe had also painstakingly constructed the seed trays with wooden sides, usually from wood found in skips along the roadside, with wire-netting bases so they will drain easily and not get waterlogged. The polytunnel was a companion to our shop, which is open from 10 a.m. until noon every Sunday from late February until early November.

The shop is a long, large shipping container which I found in *Construction News* in Hammersmith public library. We bought it for £1,200 from a firm in Derby, who brought it down on a long loader at no extra cost. It was a memorable day, because of the sheer skill of the driver. It arrived late one autumn afternoon, and when we saw it out-s ide in the road, we thought the driver would never be able to get the lorry through our gates and swing it around to where we wanted it, just behind a small tree right at the back of this part of the Perryn site, so it would not take up any valuable land.

The driver was in his early sixties and only about five foot tall, yet was incredibly strong, reminding me of the diminutive weightlifter, Precious McKenzie. First of all he paced a distance up the road, to work out how he would back the lorry through the gates, just like a fast bowler pacing out his run, before starting his first over. Even then, as the lorry folded away from his cab it seemed he would bring down the nearest lamppost, but he cleared this by twelve inches, before dropping the back of the lorry neatly backwards through the gate. We gave him a round of applause: 'I've never had that before,' he said cheerfully in a rich northern accent. His next feat was even more impressive as he fixed metal chains from the container's rooftop hooks to the crane on his cab. He swung it perfectly without damaging the tree which was inches away, as the huge container rose above us and then down onto the ground that had been prepared for it. A perfect job and a man to admire.

The reason that we had invested in the steel shipping container, which we then painted green, was that our previous shed on the edge of the Vale estate had been burned down twice, and as a result the bill for insuring it in the future had risen to a massive £1,000 yearly, which we thought was precious money wasted. It had also been regularly burgled. You would need a tank to smash your way into our shipping container, the double doors of which had not one but two padlocks.

The shipping container, now home for our shop, not only provides all our needs at lower prices than would be paid at garden centres, but also a weekly meeting place for the members, where they can talk, swap stories and ideas, and generally fulfil the very important community side of allotment gardening. John Roberts and Doreen are on weekly duty, helped by others, and outside is always Joe Hughes dressed in his Sunday best in preparation for his walk later down the Uxbridge Road to the Coningham.

*　　　*　　　*

Joe came from Mayo many years ago and worked on sites around the London area. Although retired for some years, he spends nearly all day on the Perryn and Chestnuts sites not only working on his own plot, but doing whatever is needed for the whole site. He is an expert shed builder, and his own shed houses a large gas ring, linked to a Calor gas container, upon which the kettle is boiled for our lunchtime tea, or to heat up lunch. Not only can he recall every job he was on during his working life, and what went right or wrong, but like the rest of the Irish men on our site he knows the ancestry of every Irish person in our neighbourhood. I mentioned to him that I'd been to Mary's pub in Deal, and she'd remarked that she used to work in a pub in Shepherd's Bush, close to Acton. Joe not only knew of her, but also her past, which village she came from in Ireland and to whom she was related, and how her brother was now a wealthy hotel owner in Ireland. The Data Protection Act obviously does not apply to the Irish memory bank. If surprised while sitting alone in his shed, Joe can usually be found listening to a radio station from Dublin.

The actual construction of the polytunnel took several weeks, as everything had to be level and measured after each move with a spirit level. Finally, a non-windy day had to be chosen for the large covering to be put over the framework. It had a door at one end, built by Joe, and an opening at the other in readiness for the hot weather, so that the air could go straight through the tunnel and cool it down.

The really painstaking work was not the construction, which had been going on for some time, but the choosing, ordering and planting of the seeds in the seed trays. A fiddly job at the best of times. John Roberts had done all the planting, because he is the most patient of us all. I am afraid I am not so patient!

John Roberts is our treasurer and is also in charge of the shop. John is now in his seventies and is a remarkable man, full of generosity, which no doubt comes from his life as a practising Christian. He is very involved with the church, and is never available on Saturdays because of his involvement with the music and choirs. He has a special knowledge of growing certain vegetables dating back to his boyhood in the Caribbean, and is the master at growing peppers and corn on the cob, always placing two plants very close to each other when planting them, and he is certainly rewarded with the best of crops.

After the long dark depressing days and nights of winter comes the more pleasant, although busy, period of the year, when I ring Chrissie at Tuckers, our seed merchants in Devon, and arrange the date for the delivery of potatoes and all the other seeds, plants, and fertilisers we need to stock the shop for the coming season.

We usually reopen the shop in the last week in February, and start selling enormous amounts of the twelve or more varieties of potato, as well as onion and shallot sets, large quantities of organic compost, and seeds, which we buy in bulk and re-packet for 50p. It is extraordinary how the price of seeds has rocketed in the shops recently, to a point where the price is double for half the amount of seed.

However, there is always a snag with the Tuckers' delivery. For some reason they have signed a rather complicated contract which means that the company that picks up the goods from them in Devon cannot deliver direct to us, but has to transfer its load to another firm based on the outskirts of London. Every year they are instructed to ring us and tell us an approximate time of delivery. They sometimes do, but it never equates with what actually happens. It is all rather frustrating, because Joe, Charlie Rycroft and John waste a lot of their time just hanging about in the hope that the delivery lorry will arrive.

Charlie Rycroft is another Irishman, originally from Sligo in the west of Ireland, who lives overlooking the Perryn site, and he has the important task of keeping the key to the main gate. Despite being in his mid-eighties, he manages to do sterling work for the society as a whole, even perching on top of a ladder as he snips the top off the long hedge that runs along the road guarding the Perryn site. But as Joe says, 'It's the working that keeps him alive.' So it is with many of our older members as long as their limbs stay sound! Charlie will always help dig someone's plot if they are in a bit of medical trouble, and his own plot is always first to be completely dug, autumn and spring.

Tuckers' delivery finally turns up last thing on Thursday evening. Luckily Joe and Charlie are still there. Every year I vow to find our own trucking company to transfer this large order from the West Country direct to us within the day.

One of our other regular deliveries is from the Compost Company. They are excellent and always arrive within half an hour of their estimation. Our Compost delivery arrives the next day, and we are able to pile high two lots of compost; the organic, and an all-purpose but more expensive version which sells just as well. There is usually a week between the delivery and opening the shop, so John can price everything. He is quite amazing at this and carries a lot of figures in his head, and can remember how much the wholesale price was several years ago. Chrissie wisely stores everything in her computer and is able to tell us what we have previously ordered and at what price. The combination of Chrissie's wholesaling and John's shop keeping is the perfect. All I have to do is place the order.

John is regularly helped on Sunday mornings by Doreen, who has a plot on another of our sites known as the Goldsmiths about a quarter of a mile away. John usually runs her back there, or to her home, when he finally locks the two large padlocks of the shipping container. The Goldsmiths site has twelve plots and boasts a long brick wall that has a conservation order placed on it. It is one of the five sites which make up our Association. Geographically they form quite a tight circle around East Acton, and all the sites could be visited within a gentle half-hour walk.

Doreen is always having to appeal for more members to work in the shop with her and John especially as in the future a lot of John's time on a Sunday morning will be taken up with selling plants from the polytunnel, thus leaving Doreen alone in the shop.

So we will put notices up asking for volunteers, if only for two hours: what is that in a whole year? Two of our newer arrivals, Kathryn and Jayne, are offering quite regular appearances and enjoying the experience. They're known as the BBC girls because they both work in the subtitling division.

Doreen always brings a flask of coffee with her, and biscuits, which she will tempt you with if you arrive at the right moment. It is always nice to have a cup of coffee half way through a Sunday morning. Rowing training as a cox occupies me on Saturday and Sunday mornings and two evenings a week, but I do manage to get to my plot for what is left of the weekend, and a couple of nights a week, for an hour or so. It is amazing what you can achieve on an allotment with only an hour a day. Sometimes when I get fed up with my work at home I tell my wife Juliet, 'just going up to the allotment,' or as my daughter Gemma used to call it when younger the 'lop lop'.

To keep people in touch, we are going to put up notice-boards at the entrance to each site. Unfortunately, not many of our members are on the Internet, although more and more allotment information is to be found there free of charge, a challenge to gardening magazines that cost £3 or more a time.

In the middle of all these annual worries comes a piece of good news. The Ealing Community Chest Rolling Fund has granted us £1,000 after our application for three new sheds for women members, and money to build new noticeboards. The noticeboards have been made at cost by one of our members, and it was agreed we could spend the rest of the money on cleaning and repainting the outside of our shipping container shop. Years of salt underneath has caused the paint to peel and we want to smarten it up.

We have had one grant in the past, for £5,000, for the installation of the new water system and seven new sheds. Self-built allotment sheds have character, but I ordered new ones for the new ground we were given by the Park Club. I thought as it looked onto their ground it would be a good neighbourly act to put up smart, uniform sheds. These grants must be seen to be focusing on ethnic minorities, the coming together of the community. We fulfil both these roles.

I am in favour of smaller grants, because it is much harder bidding for the really large sums, and as we do most of our own work, we need the money for the hardware itself. Sheds are quite expensive when bought but we get ours from a sawmill just outside Reading called New Line Sheds. They are a charming old-world company with an exceptional telephone manner, and they deliver more or less at the time they say they will, free of charge.

We have introduced a rule that those who are awarded these sheds must remember that they remain the property of the Acton Gardening Association, and therefore must be treated with creosote or some other preservative once a year.

For the first day at the shop I buy Cherie and Pink Fir Apple potatoes. Later I will buy some more main crop Romano from Tuckers, because there is such a run on them. Normally, Desiree are the most popular. Our annual seed potato order comes to nearly £1,000 every year, because we get orders from allotment holders in other parts of the borough who do not have a shop. I also buy a bag of general compost, as this is what I use to sow some of my seeds in.

The cockatoos are back. We first spotted

them about a year ago: green parrot-like creatures, who travel together, as if for protection against attack from other birds. There are all sorts of rumours as to how they arrived here. Some say they escaped from Heathrow airport while in transit, or from someone's house, or a zoo. I first found a pair on the towpath between Hammersmith and Putney, where there was a tree broken in half by a strike of lightning. They had settled down inside and bred, and were quite an attraction for the families taking their Sunday walk, or those of us on the way to rowing on the Hard at Putney.

Now here were at least eight more, using one of the tallest trees on our allotment, screeching very loudly, swooping off together like some foreign air force and then returning. The crows, big and black and heavy, did not seem to like them much, but they were too slow to catch these bright green, streamlined, high-speed flyers. At least they don't seem to feed off anything from our plots, although I do wonder how they survive and what they eat. Our major quarrel with nature is the pigeons, or more accurately the ring doves, some of whom nest in the yew tree above John Johnson's and my plot, and, when we have gone, swoop down to peck to bits anything they want.

Every year these marauders catch me out for being too casual and not netting my broccoli.

They will attack greens from the day they are planted to the day they have grown three feet tall. Yet they won't eat some things at all. Broad beans, for example, are quite safe. If you want to guarantee the future of your greens you have to put nets over and around them, which is a pity because netting is not attractive. Then I remind myself I am on an allotment and not in a manicured garden.

There are various other theories about how to keep birds at bay. Mike Mallett, the Kent fruit farmer and grower who comes to the weekly Hammersmith farmers' market, says that beer cans strung up are quite a good thing, because they make a noise the birds don't like. I told him that I thought our London pigeons and ring doves, who come from France originally, were quite used to the noise of a city and would not be put off by a few rattling beer cans as they might in rural Kent. I have seen people hang up old CDs, which flash in the light, and certainly the old country idea of black cotton strung around a row of peas seems to work. Why is it that the birds like peas, but not broad beans? They certainly do not like black cotton, presumably because they can't see it until they touch it and can't work it out so they wisely leave well alone.

The robins are only interested in closely following your digging, and finding tiny insects the human eye can't see, besides the occasional worm small enough for them to make off with. Thrushes do much the same, although they are much shyer, and are adept at cracking snails open with their beaks using a handy stone as an anvil. The blackbird sings a lot and behaves very well until the strawberries and raspberries mature, when he has the annoying habit of sinking his beak into the fruit and taking just a slice for himself, preferring to leave the rest for us growers with a telltale hole in it.

In general all the birds seem capable of stripping a cherry tree of all its fruit on the very day it has ripened, as well as doing the same with redcurrants, although the blackcurrants are not so popular. This is nature, and we exist together. A good allotment adage is always plant a bit more than you need, so that there is something left for the birds.

*   *   *

One drawback about working on an allotment is that you become very suspicious of visitors you do not know. We should be welcoming folk but have learned to be cautious from previous experience. Hence, one spring day I was approaching our new side gate when a white van drew up, immediately arousing my suspicions about fly-tipping. We have suffered from this in the past when a lorry smashed through our frail wooden gates and dumped masses of rubble and earth at the back of our shop. Fly-tipping is on the increase in the inner cities, because of the gradual filling of landfill sites on the outskirts, and the cost of properly getting rid of waste. Fortunately, on investigation, he turned out to be a fellow allotmenteer, who came from Hounslow and was doing a grass-cutting job nearby and wondered if we would like the grass. After I'd put him through a third degree of questioning, which, on reflection, seemed rather rude, I got Joe to come and open the main gates.

He had had the grass in the back of his van in black bags for some time, and it had already begun to smell, but quite healthily, with the heat it was creating. It would be just right to be thrown into compost bins, or at this moment onto the communal manure heap. He told us the problems his own association were having with their allotments in Hounslow. The council had outsourced the running of allotments to a private company and some of the ground in his locality had been poisoned, either by asbestos, or something worse dumped on it years before.

We also have our own form of antisocial behaviour right here on our site. John Roberts says that people, he knows not who, keep dumping their rubbish onto the ground that he is clearing in the hollow next to the Virgin health club site, which backs onto the Park

Club. It is infuriating for him because, as fast as he cleans the land to get it ready for growing in the coming season, someone else comes along and dumps all their weeds, or worse, on it.

When John started work at the back of the Perryn site, it was totally barren and overgrown, in use as a dump, and had various trees lying across it. Gradually he has brought it back to life, with a huge amount of work. His own plot is on the Bromyard Avenue site, but he is going to grow potatoes, beans, corn and pumpkins, bringing this piece of land back to life. So the fact that people still come and dump their waste on land he has cleared bothers him a lot, and I don't blame him.

In an attempt to cure all this eco-vandalism Joe and I say we will start a communal compost heap, where everyone can put their weeds, and we will add manure and rotting grass to help it along the way. Within a year there should be some good compost for everyone to use, and John will be happily able to continue cultivating what I refer to as 'the new Palestine'.

I am always interested to know what other allotment organisations are doing and I have regular chats on the phone with Stephen Cole, who now works for Ealing borough council, and runs all their allotments. He has some alarming news. He says that he is in danger of losing forty plots to the Crossrail scheme that would bring trains around London, from west to east, despite the fact that there is a line that already does this. The council did not tell him about it and have backed the scheme, which makes it very difficult for him to oppose it. A case of the right hand not knowing what the left hand is doing, which seems quite common in local councils.

At home I have been planting a few boxes of early lettuce, in readiness for the coming rowing season when I might have to get my weight back down to 8 stone 8 lbs if I get a boat for the Henley Royal Regatta. At the moment I am with the students' novice boat at Imperial College and hover on a winter weight of nine stone. As I am five feet seven and a half inches tall, I reckon my natural weight would be anything up to ten stone.

In addition to lettuce, I sow boxes of basil and start growing moss curled English parsley indoors for the first time, because it never seems to germinate when I put it straight into the soil outdoors. I am also about to start my great personal sowing experiment of the season; growing parsnips indoors, and when they are big enough, transplanting them out into the open. Having never read anything about this I wonder if it will work. We will soon see, but I am fed up with sowing a whole packet of parsnip seeds in the recommended way: put your dibber into the ground and make a hole; fill it with compost; put three parsnip seeds into the compost; water; choose the strongest plant to grow and throw away the other two. Well, it has not worked for me. So now I am pre-planting them in a box indoors in the warm. No more of that wretched nine-week wait for germination. This is sink or swim time for my parsnips!

I have also put some mint seed into a tray, and hope that will come up, because I seem to have lost all the mint I transplanted from Jerome's site last year. I thought mint was meant to be indestructible! Usually people cannot get rid of it as it roots deeply and spreads everywhere. Mine did not. So I am growing it in a controlled area, and then I will plant it out, either into its own large pot or straight into the ground.

Both fresh mint and parsnips have a quality that you can never buy in the shops. The trouble with so much shop food is that although it is sold as 'fresh' it has probably travelled halfway up and down a motorway since it was harvested. The beauty of allotment food is that you pick it just before the ten-minute walk home, and what a difference it makes to the sweetness and juiciness of a parsnip, or to the smell and tanginess of mint.

I am convinced that indoor growing is the way to go, because you can control everything, and then choose the moment to harden them off outside on the patio to accustom the plants to an outdoor life, before they are planted out on the allotment.

I have a full box of Webb's Wonder lettuce. I grew some last year and it was nice and crisp in the middle, but because I have stupidly put all the seed in the same box this year it will all come at once. However, when I put the first lot out, there was no danger of that. All the plants 'melt', just disappear with the cold. Or I think it is the cold. I did put an offcut of the polytunnel's plastic around a second lot but they disappeared too. So it is back to planting another tray at home. Not a good start to my growing season!

They always tell you that your potatoes should go in on St Patrick's Day, 17th March. I am not sure who decreed this, but it obviously emanated from Ireland. This year it was too wet to carry out this ritual. It is no good putting potatoes in too early if the soil is wet and cold. They will just rot, and that will be that. So I wait. But for how long, that is the trick. I shall just follow Joe. He buys several sacks of potatoes, on behalf of friends on his other plot in West Ealing, which he fills mainly with potatoes and onions.

It is also time to prepare some land for the spring planting of broad beans. My autumn sowing has been desecrated by the various freeze-ups in the winter. Unusual, but a fact. I think they were too forward when they were hit by the first freeze-up. Still, I will have enough for more than a meal or two.

Debra is one of our most skilful growers. She comes from the Suffolk countryside, and can cultivate anything. She is very busy at her job and proves that a little work, but often, really can make an allotment work for you. She sometimes comes at dawn, scurries around and then gets back into her bright orange van before going to work. I meet her, as busy as ever, filling her greenhouse with all sorts of seeds in boxes, and she gives me some climbing French bean seeds and some 'old-fashioned' sweet pea seeds. I remember the sweet peas climbing up her beans last year, which had a really good effect on the otherwise rather boring runner bean frame. It takes the imagination of a Debra to do something like that.

Debra also gave me a clump of raspberries she is thinning out. For some reason raspberry canes cost a lot when you order them from a seed firm, even though they are prolific, and when you send away for them they never seem to take. Whether they do not like my soil or not I do not know, but I don't say no to the offer from Debra.

I've read that raspberries don't like much interference and that they can grow almost wild, which is what has really happened to the plot of land I originally set aside for them. Now grass has grown everywhere around them, and to a neater gardener it must look like one of those overgrown pieces of land which local authorities obligingly label 'conservation' areas. They produce more fruit when grown this way. However, next season I vow to weed them right through and set up a clean raspberry patch. Different pruning is required for the late and early varieties. The ordinary raspberry just has its old wood cut away, whereas later fruiting raspberries are cut right to the ground. I have an awful feeling that in the autumn I did it the wrong way around.

On a lovely warm spring Sunday, I went to the car boot sale at the Chiswick Community School in search of a rake. I really needed one, and usually there are plenty of old tools about, but not this Sunday. Two sisters always bring plants that they have propagated and grown themselves. I always buy some plants from them: two for the garden at home and at least one for the flower area in front of my shed on the allotment. We always have a long talk about plants, and allotment and life in general. Frankly I never know the names of the flowers I am about to buy, and they keep a large book in the back of the car so that they can show you what they will look like when they are fully grown. I bought a honeysuckle to wind around the small tree that I can see out of my shed window. The rest of the day I surprised myself by actually digging around the raspberry area, and making room for the canes that Debra had given me. She was in and out as quickly as usual this morning, but despite her hurry managed to drop in on the way to do something in her greenhouse, as well as her plot. Such energy and organisation! She is always giving me something, and at long last I was able to return the favour: a clump of carnations which have grown well indoors for me at home. I plant the rest of the carnations in front of my shed. I love their smell, their elegance and their value as a buttonhole.

Watering is now needed not only for the new plants, but on the fruit trees and the tayberries, which will supply such delicious fruit in a month or so. They were recommended to me by Richard Wiltshire, my allotment guru in Deptford, and he was right. They have all the properties of the loganberry, but are much more simple to grow, turning a dark damson colour when they are ready to pick

I came in touch with Richard during our fight to keep the allotments. He is a lecturer at King's College, and has guided the allotment movement in Deptford, setting up a very good website. He has also guided the government by working on a Good Practice Guide for allotments, and has represented the allotment movement well with politicians. One of his strengths is his ability to act as devil's advocate at allotment gatherings. He will drop a verbal depth charge by asking: 'What right do we have to allotments, when houses are needed so badly?' You can hear him telling his students 'discuss and decide'. He speaks fluent Japanese and has a great love of that country, where he says there is a serious allotment movement, with the cost of an allotment sometimes as high as £2,000 a year because of the lack of land. I wonder if they miniaturise everything as they do with bonsai? If ever I have a problem, I ring Richard, a very civilised person.

Debra returns and reminds me that my new fruit trees will need a lot of water as they begin to settle in. They will not provide any fruit this year, but must be looked after for their future fruit bearing. I bought the tayberries very cheaply at Homebase as they were half dead. It is always worth buying their rejects, if you need them, and then throwing lots of water at them. After a few months they usually pick up. It is remarkable the recovery powers of nature.

I have some loganberries, but they have become part of an even worse waste area of the plot than the raspberries which started next to them. However, I made a pile of rubbish in the middle of some wild blackberry bushes which I wanted to encourage because they have a high production rate. I wanted to make their presence look purposeful, in case anyone started criticising the state of the secretary's plot. I am sure my plot would never pass an inspection, but it does produce, and I'm a rather eccentric producer. The loganberries were looked upon as quite valuable by my Italian next door neighbour Angelo, who asked his Italian friend Benito to get a root for him, which he did. I think he now has a successful loganberry. Mine are fighting their way through the weeds and blackberries, although they do seem happier like this. I should really tidy this area up one day, but would have to sacrifice a large part of the blackberry crop. Angelo was a restaurateur for many years, including running the well-known Stock Pot in the King's Road. He cooked and ended up running several restaurants. He has retired now, but his wife continues to work He is a very gentle, soft-voiced person, who loves his plot, and is often to be found sitting out beneath a large fig tree he has grown. On a hot day he could be back in Italy. He often looks across our small divide, and we have a chat.

One side of my plot is bordered by a wooden fence, which encloses the garden of a newly renovated house. I have planted some new fruit trees along the fence, and between them put in some rhubarb plants grown from seed. I really like rhubarb, which can be improved in the cooking with a mixture of oranges or ginger, or both, and brown sugar. There are rumours that it is unsafe to eat rhubarb in certain months. I have not dropped dead doing this, but their leaves are definitely poisonous, and can be used as a killing liquid in the garden when boiled. Some people also add the nicotine of cigarette ends but I prefer not to. However, I don't think it would rid the plot of bindweed. The only cure for this is to dig down several feet to find its source, like finding oil.

Richard Wiltshire's other gardening advice was to grow asparagus, but I have tried this in the past without much success. There is nothing to beat English asparagus, but it has a very short season, and it takes up a lot of ground. Once you have planted an asparagus bed it is there for a long time. You cannot plant anything else there apart from a few salad seeds. But I found it very fussy and, because weeds are attracted by anything dormant where there's no digging action, careful weeding is necessary.

An asparagus bed is started by planting the asparagus crowns almost straightaway as they are very dry if they are sent to you through the post. They look rather like an octopus with its tentacles hanging down. Tuckers' latest charge was fifty crowns for £39. Harvesting is not done for the first or second year so the whole thing is a very lengthy process. But if you have a wedge of ground that's well fed with compost, that you do not want to touch again, apart from keeping it clear of weeds, then asparagus is for you.

Meanwhile, watering has to be continued. It is early days yet, but Thames Water claim it has been the driest winter for years, and yet it seemed to me that every weekend it had rained at some point, and spoilt my wish to dig.

*　　　*　　　*

It is time to plant the first two rows of French Breakfast radish this season, together with two rows of spring onion, but they are almost under the yew tree so I do not expect much success. I have lunchtime tea with Joe and Steve, whom I always think of as the potato expert. He continually says, 'To keep a long story short', and he has many stories from his homeland of Ireland. The talk otherwise is about the rotten local Labour council, the rotten Mayor of London, Ken Livingstone, and the rotten Congestion charge, which Joe says is about to creep further out, as he knows men who have been measuring things right up to the roundabout leading into Shepherd's Bush Green. The allotment has always been a centre of information, as well as rumour. The information is usually accurate, because the Irish always know someone who is working on some site or another. Right now there are various major schemes going on to the west, like the new Wembley, which was brought to a halt because the crane drivers were threatened by marksmen. We know not why. Closer to home in Shepherd's Bush, they are constructing a massive new shopping mall, as if we need it. The men are always stopping because of the perennial health and safety fear of unexploded Second World War bombs. It seems comparatively safe here in Joe's hut, where his friendly robin has given notice that he is about to build a nest. Already there are some untidy bits of straw and grass hanging down from the corner above the seat where I sit for tea.

It seems a strange place to build a nest, because they will be able to come in and out only when Joe is there and leaves the door open. Also it is quite public. We will all know where the nest is, and usually birds are quite secretive about their nesting habits. However, over the days ahead the nest-building continues, and it is obvious eggs will eventually be laid there.

Joe, as always, has a solution to the nesting problem. He is going to cut a small square out of the side of his shed. Not too large, but just large enough for the robins to use as their own personal door at all hours. He completes the work that very afternoon. I think the robins should be grateful to him. We now leave biscuit crumbs for them on Joe's table inside the shed, instead of outside on the step as we have always done before. These birds are getting deservedly spoiled!

The only birds that build nests near my plot are the wretched ring doves in the yew tree, no doubt giving them a good view of anything green and beakworthy that comes up on my plot beneath them. There are plenty of other birds, of course, but my robins are highly secretive when not following me as I dig, when they will stand almost on my feet. Wrens used to build and hide in the huge bay tree at the end of my plot, but since Benito kindly cut it in half for me, there hasn't been much sign of nests hidden in the middle of it. John Johnson, however, who comes later in the evening than I usually do, says that he thinks wrens are nesting in there again. It has grown rapidly again, and thicker, which is good for secretive birds like wrens.

John Johnson is one of our new members. If only they were all like him. Industrious, always improving something or other. A wonderful carpenter. Everything that I am not. His wife is an artist, and has been up to the allotment to do some drawings. I gather she teaches art. I can never quite make out exactly what John does, because I am not that nosey, but I think he looks after properties for important and wealthy Arabs.

He already has one neat shed, on the plot beside me, that he has painted a tasteful dark green so that it blends with its surroundings. Now he is building another, and plans his answer to the polytunnel as well. He always asks permission to make an improvement, and you can trust that his work will be tasteful.

Suddenly the peace and hope of spring is broken by a terrible misunderstanding. One day Debra asks if I want yet another compost bin. Predictably I say 'yes'. She tells me to take away an old green construction at the end of her greenhouse plot. It was made in the days when it was fashionable to swivel compost boxes over every few weeks, a method I would never recommend or use. Why turn compost? The whole thing is to let it rot down like a good muck heap. Still, I did empty all the earth out of it, and put it together with my other boxes. I first heard of impending trouble, needless to say, from Joe, who enquired if I'd seen a green compost box that had gone missing from Les's plot. It answered the description of the box that I had removed.

I had a rather empty feeling of fear in my stomach. I hoped Les had not discovered the box on my site before I could explain the situation. That, however, was not to be. By the time I met him some days later he was beside himself with rage. I owned up immediately and explained how it had happened. This did not seem to mitigate the crime in his mind. He said that he had spent several years filling the box, that it had been ruined, that it had been on his site all the time and that Debra had no right to give it away. Although, secretly, in my mind I begged to differ, nothing I could say would soften the situation at the moment. When he'd gone I returned the box and tried to put as much of the earth back in it as possible. After several more apologies he accepted the situation, and we were able to talk together again without any rancour on his behalf. It was one of those allotment situations I wish I could have avoided. Holding office as the Honorable Secretary made it even worse.

There was a wonderful feeling within me once all this nastiness had passed over. I am not built for rows! I hate telling people not to do something in my role as honorary secretary. That is why I have encouraged the committee to relax a lot of the stricter rules of the past. Sometimes matters have to be addressed, and you do get your pet hates. It is only human. Mine is the over-use of hoses, because the water bill is our biggest loss of revenue. People, unbelievably, leave their hoses running into their potato patches, which I think is a waste. Paola has returned from Italy and told me that her father told her never to water the tomatoes. I do believe too much watering of everything increases the tops rather than the roots. Tomatoes do not need as much water as we think, because many plants starved of water will go deeper to find it. Yet when it gets very hot I like to give them something as well as a feed. Fruit also needs watering, as do to lettuce and carrots

The first black bag full of fresh grass clippings arrives over the hedge from my Scottish neighbours. We usually have a chat about the weather, and the goings-on at the council, and their new next door neighbours. The grass that comes over the fence is already warm from being kept in the black plastic sack, and I unload it into one of my compost bins, pushing it well down. It is wonderful for compost, as long as no chemicals have been used on it before it was cut. Grass from sports fields is particularly prone to this, and should be avoided.

Compost-making has become an obsession with me. I have yet to produce the finished article, because this is the first year I have assembled my collection of bins and filled them. However, I have been bringing supermarket bags of household waste to put in the compost bins throughout the winter, and all my home output of urine, which is still not appreciated by either my wife or daughter. The more of nature we return to itself the better, which is why I would like to be buried right here on the allotment in the land in front of my shed, in a cardboard coffin. Just think what climbing beans and sweet peas my remains could produce. Could this be the start of the organic world's answer to global warming?

Joe's robins have come over all shy. When

we go into his shed for tea, even though they have seen us all winter, and were willing to hop into the shed to peck at bread and biscuit crumbs, they will not enter while we are there. The nest is built, and the mother sitting. But they fly about outside, land on the step, or even on their own open square of a door, stand there on their matchstick-like legs, eye us suspiciously and go away again. Only when we go back to our own work do they deign to re-enter. They must know we would never harm them, or pry into the nest, which is a right straggly mess, hanging a quarter of the way down the wall, all wisps of grass and hay. The actual nest, presumably, is all tight and neat above this mess. Perhaps this is part of their cunning plan to pretend there is no nest at all, and the mess is meant as camouflage.

The planting season really gathers pace, although I still think I am tempting fate, because despite the lack of rain the ground has not warmed up properly. But, like everyone else, I have no patience and set out to fill the newly dug earth.

First in are sixty red onions surrounded by sixty-six shallots. I prefer shallots to onions, but I like red onions because they are mild-flavoured and can be eaten raw. I now know why French chefs always use shallots in their cooking, and never white onions as the British do. Shallots blend into a meal without dominating it. There was a time when I used

49

to pickle some of my shallots, and I might well do a bottle or two this year. I was quite impressed by some homemade pickled onions using balsamic vinegar in the winter at the Chiswick farmers' market. I will try the same recipe with shallots, because the vinegar usually used for pickling is a bit sharp, and could dominate the taste of the shallots.

Joe offered me some rhubarb plants grown from seed by Debra. I take three and put them in between the recently planted fruit trees. At least they will get regular watering where they are. There was some late purple sprouting broccoli and the last of the leeks to harvest. I never grow large leeks, preferring them to be almost pencil thin, which isn't at all the style of allotment growers.

It is now the culmination of the winter rowing season, and for the first time a commercial radio station, LBC, has bought the rights to the university Boat Race, and appointed me as their rowing correspondent and, on the great day itself, the co-commentator on the race. When, as a little boy, I listened to John Snagge as he said the memorable words by way of description 'In out, in out', I never thought that one day I would be doing his job. The drawback is all this sudden activity on and around the nearby River Thames keeps me away from my plot when I should be really busy.

Once the Boat Race is over I spend a couple

of days down in Deal with my friend Joe Steeples, and his wife Julie, before getting back into a routine. I start by planting my potatoes, Cherie, Pink Fir Apple and Romano. None of my usual favourite Charlotte this year, because I forgot to order any! A big mistake. My own compost is not ready so I put a handful of Growmore around each potato. As I will be eating very few of the potatoes I am planting, the whole exercise does not interest me that much, but it will take up a lot of my land, which is quite useful when I cannot come regularly to the allotment. The only time I really enjoy them is when I roast them in my special way on a Sunday evening. I parboil them, cut them into small pieces, sometimes scatter chopped rosemary and garlic over them and bake them on a tray drizzled in olive oil. They come out crisp and delicious.

Meanwhile Joe reports that the robins for which he built their own entrance into his shed have turned very odd indeed. They are nesting and entering his shed whenever they like through the square he has cut away for them, but they have started being rather unpleasant. Not at all like those sweet robins, who perch on the covers of Christmas cards. He says that they have taken to flying into the shed through the open door when he is sitting there, either having his lunchtime sandwich or just listening to Dublin radio, and aim straight at his face, fortunately colliding with his glasses. They have also taken to flying at his neck and pecking it, when he is opening up his shed, and yesterday they even followed him one hundred yards down the path buzzing him like fighter pilots in a wartime skirmish. One day I am sitting having tea in my seat under the nest when I get a winging from one of the robins who purposely flies against my face. All this aggression is quite frightening, even though it does come from a couple of tiny birds. But we cannot work out quite why they have changed.

In contrast, at our end of the allotments John Johnson and I have become enraptured by the blackbird that has stayed in our area for some time. He sings as if specially for us, and flies very short distances between our two plots so that he is always around us. We cannot work out where he is nesting but he will rest near us for some time just singing to us, and then work the earth in search of worms and other insects. What a difference from Joe's robins. He is a thoroughly nice fellow.

I take another week away from the plot for an intensive, intermediate cookery course at the Prue Leith school in Kensington, now run by Caroline Waldegrave. I've always done some cooking, but not really understood it, and also lacked confidence. When they hear I have allotments, one in Juliet's name and one in my own, they are envious about what I can grow, as they use a lot of fresh produce. I gain confidence in cooking, but it also deepens my respect for the allotments that can provide so much decent food in these times of instant, supermarket, air-miled, tasteless ingredients. It makes me want to grow more herbs than I do at present, like basil, rocket, oregano, thyme, mint, parsley and coriander.

I find that upstairs in my conservatory on the front of my office is best for growing herbs, but they start to grow well out of doors towards the end of spring. I interviewed an old-fashioned Yorkshire farmer just north of Huddersfield, who told me of an interesting partnership he now had with Asian allotment holders there. They use coriander nearly every day in their curries, but because of the amount they needed and the restrictive size of their plots they eventually came to an agreement with him to plant twelve acres of coriander on his farm, paying him a rental for the land. He was amazed at the way they cropped it, very quickly with special knives, and that they get at least two crops a year. The enterprise has enlarged now, and they are wholesaling it into Bradford fruit and vegetable market.

So you had this Yorkshire-accented farmer, who had been farming there for years, with his new Asian clients, and they all had tea together regularly in his farmhouse kitchen, and got on as if they had been together all their lives. They had been joined together by a mutual respect for and love of the land. The same element that draws together our diverse group of people from seventeen different countries.

When I first took over a plot in the mid-1980s the growing of flowers was frowned upon, apart from chrysanthemums, or anything that could be entered into a show. Gradually I have turned the whole square in front of my shed into a flowerbed, with a few cucumbers, and tomatoes, and a wigwam of French climbing beans, growing at the end by the path. In my conservatory at home I have already been nursing a box of carnations, as well as statice grown from seed. Statice supplies colour in the house through the winter, if dried and hung up first of all. When I first started out on the allotment, as flowers were not encouraged, I had never taken much interest in them, although in those days Juliet regularly cultivated her plot, and was the great flower grower, with me concentrating on vegetables. But now with her here less and less my interest in growing flowers has increased, and I like to take a bunch home in the evening so that they can fill our home with colour.

In the boxes of tomatoes I am growing at home, I have already done my usual trick and muddled them up, so when it comes to planting them out I will not know my Alicante from my Gardener's Delight.

After a mere three weeks the time has come for the second part of my great parsnip experiment, as the moment comes to transfer them to my plot. The trouble is knowing the right moment. How long the roots should be? How tall the tops should be? Anyway, I put all-purpose compost in the rows, poke my finger in to make a hole and drop the tiny rooted parsnip plants down in the hole, before soaking each one with a full can of water. The whole experiment will be interesting. As will John Johnson's experiment with carrots. He aims to transplant the seedlings into the soil outdoors when the weather really warms up.

Since my Prue Leith experience I have become aware of the importance of spinach, or the cut-and-come-again leaf beet that I grow. It is a basic for the pasta that I have been taught to make, and it goes perfectly with ricotta cheese for ravioli. I have always grown a row or two but now I am taking out all the old spinach that is rapidly going to seed, almost before I can pick a few leaves. I put them on John Johnson's wheelbarrow and take a couple of loads over to the hens on Benito's plot, which is looked after by Paola. I thread as much as I can through the wire, which the hens peck at greedily. I pile the rest up for Paola when she feeds them in the morning.

The chickens are going to benefit from greens that have turned to seed, such as broccoli, which has fed me well, but is now over. The hens like this greenery as much as the spinach, and again I feed them a little bit through the wire, trying to make sure they all get a fair share. The hens do look really well, and happy. Every now and again if you remain very quiet towards the evening you can see a forlorn fox sitting on the mound above them just gazing at them. This does not seem to worry the hens, who peck away at the ground as usual, probably knowing that they are quite safe with all the protection above and below ground.

I have observed that chickens are quite intelligent, contrary to their image. After all one of the worst remarks you can make about a panicking human being is that they are 'running around like a headless chicken'. Well, I know from my country experiences that chickens do run around after their heads have been chopped off until they die. But I daresay if you beheaded a human being they wouldn't do too well.

Anyway I think these hens are quite bright and calm. Paola has started letting her favourite hen out with her as she is weeding or digging, and it stays just behind her as a dog would, pecking away finding interesting bits of grit and insects. It even allows her to stroke it. It does not try to leave the plot.

Unfortunately, the committee have already noticed one or two plots that are not being used properly. This is really annoying so soon in the season considering the length of our waiting list, and the almost daily calls I take from people pleading for a plot. Time and again John, Joe and I wonder why some people take on an allotment and then ignore it. What's the point?

The plot belonging to my wife and I—which I now spend the most time looking after as the demands of the home and our daughter Gemma, who is in her late-teens, keep my wife busy enough—is not tidy, and maybe would not pass an inspection if it was owned by the council. But I go there a lot, potter about a lot, and it produces a lot.

I am still digging patches here and there that I will soon need. And in the conservatory at home I am busier planting more than ever before. A box of marigolds to put in among my broad beans in the organic belief that they will keep away the black fly; basil and rocket for future salads, as well as courgettes, and at last I am moving my tomatoes outside onto the patio to harden off, though they are all mixed up by now, due to my inefficiency. It is a problem knowing when to harden things off in the spring, because the temperature can drop without warning, and frost lurks, which I can see in the morning on the tiles of the roofs opposite my bedroom window.

The tale of the robins continues, as Joe reports more attacks this morning as he was opening his shed. One of them dive-bombed him and pecked his neck. The normally calm Joe is getting a bit annoyed with them, and admits to lashing out at one with his cap in frustration, but fortunately he missed. This is getting like Hitchcock's film *The Birds*.

Whilst I am sitting in Joe's shed with him Debra comes by, hurrying as usual. You almost expect her to have a worm in her mouth ready to feed someone, she is so bird-like and active. While she is talking to us we note that one robin is hopping about outside with a small worm in its beak, and one bird is actually sitting on the nest, but hidden. I stand on tiptoe so that I can have a real look inside the nest. There is a squeaking noise coming from the nest, so we presume there are now chicks, but none of us knows how long it is before they will leave the nest and their parents leave us in peace. Suddenly Debra notes that there are now two robins hopping about outside with insects in their beaks. We hadn't seen the babysitter leave the nest, so now it is deserted. What is going on? We all decide to get on with our work and leave the robins to it. I'm not so sure I'll be buying any Christmas cards in future with robins on their cover.

Although it has turned colder, and watering is needed, I decide it is time to plant my tomatoes, having hardened them off at home. There are about forty to be planted and in my local charity shop I have just bought a copy of Lindsey Bareham's *The Big Red Book of Tomatoes*. There is every possible recipe for the use of tomatoes, and one in particular that I had in a restaurant many years ago and have tried to repeat ever since, but never found the recipe: toasted bruschetta with tomatoes, rocket and garlic. Apart from the bread, everything can be home produced.

I have prepared plenty of sticks for use later, as stakes for my fifty or more tomato plants, once they start growing taller. I have gathered many of them out of skips along the way. So much good wood is being wasted these days. I also plant a square of Webb's Wonder lettuce having lost all the earlier ones, which melted away. These are bigger, and the weather just that bit better than it was a month or so ago. But I have to admit they do not look very good when I plant them, even though I hardened them for some time at home.

So everything is now set and growing towards what I hope will be a great harvest in the coming summer.

Spring Recipe

Spinach can be used all the year round, so grow several rows of cut-and-come-again leaf beet. My favourite method is to boil it in just the dampened leaves from careful washing (having removed the stalks, and used only the best parts of the leaves). Then put it in a dish, create one hole or two and crack a fresh egg into each hole. This should be cooked in a few minutes. Add grated Parmesan.

Spring/Summer

Is there one day when summer arrives? Or is it that spring just merges into summer? Certainly the weather does not change dramatically. These days you can have a heatwave in the spring or autumn.

The great gardening problem over the past year has been the dreaded tomato blight. There are all sorts of theories about it. It causes tomatoes to go brown at the top and then rot. The foliage more or less dies overnight. Two years ago I read up on it, and decided that a spray solution with copper in it was needed to prevent it. So in our Sunday shop, we stocked up on an old-fashioned remedy—Bordeaux mixture. It worked.

But what causes blight? We feel it could be the climate, as one year when there was a heatwave there was no blight. However, warm, damp and cold weather seem to encourage the scourge. When I consulted an expert, who brings tomatoes from the Isle of Wight specialist tomato farm to a farmers market in west London, as well as other markets around the South East, he told me that thunderous weather also causes blight.

It wasn't until towards the end of June that I picked my first outdoor tomatoes. Nothing had ripened, and several were beginning to look yellow and sickly. One of our Portuguese members brought back some special anti-blight mixture from his home country, and he was the only one with any decent tomatoes as a result.

On the plot next to me is one of our Italians, Giuseppe, an ex-chef with the physical bulk to prove that his food is still tasty. He has filled almost the whole of his plot with tomatoes. Once he has harvested them he reduces them to pulp, freezes the results, and uses it for the rest of the year as the main ingredient of sauces to use with pasta. For good measure he always makes his own pasta! This admission makes me highly inquisitive after my week at Leiths, where they taught us to make our own pasta. I now go to Soho to buy the right flour, but I use my own spinach. On the edge of Giuseppe's plot is a row of globe artichokes, some corn on the cob and the inevitable mass of spinach. Inevitable because the Italians eat a lot of spinach lightly fried in olive oil and mixed with garlic.

Like all our Italian plot holders he goes on holiday every summer, and assiduously weeds everything before he leaves. But I wonder why he puts all this time and effort into a tomato crop that may be at its best before his return.

I have taken a great risk by not using the Bordeaux mixture I had so painstakingly researched and recommended to everyone else. In truth I think I got a little too confident, after last year's long heatwave, which produced tons of blight-free tomatoes, or I simply forgot. I am not a great user of sprays. Although I am not strictly an organic grower, my heart and mind are. I am not fully organic because I cannot keep to the very strict Soil Association rules, like many farmers.

Conversely, I am a member of the Henry Doubleday Research Centre, now based at Ryton, near Coventry, which is the driving force behind organic gardening, started by the late Lawrence D Hills. He started the HDRA trial gardens at Bocking near Coggeshall in Essex, and wrote several books on organic gardening. Before he died I met him several times. He was one of those genuine English eccentrics, a vegan and a dedicated organic grower when it was still looked upon as odd. Most importantly for me he was the greatest expert on comfrey. It was Lawrence D Hills who found there were over one hundred different varieties and numbered them, each bearing the prefix: Bocking. The most common and widely used comfrey in gardening is Bocking 14, which has a pink flower. I have several clumps of it on my plot. It can be added to water and used as a liquid organic feed, or put into potato trenches at planting time, but more usually added as an activator to the compost bin, which is how I use it. But beware: gloves should be worn when handling it because its deceptively hairy leaves can feel like stinging nettles. It can also be put in the water butt, and the results used on tomatoes as a liquid manure. But one of our older growers, Alf Barnes, an expert on organic gardening, tells me that he finds it can be too strong for tomatoes. When I lived in the country I preferred to pour on the results of what they call duggins: the clippings off a sheep's rear still covered in manure.

Lawrence D Hills used to dry comfrey, crush it and drink it as tea. I'm afraid I don't intend to be that organic! But I do grow a very similar-looking herb called borage, which has lovely little blue flowers that please the bees. Borage leaves, and not mint, are what really should be included in a glass of Pimms. I am told by Paola that you can chop the leaves very finely and add them to an omelette. I gave Bill Geddes, our chairman, a plant this afternoon to take home. It was one of the very few really hot days so far this summer, and he'd been on his plot since eight o'clock this morning; it was mid-afternoon and he reckoned he deserved a drink.

He was the right choice for our new chairman, made at last autumn's AGM, when John Kirby, who had been our chairman for several years, had had to resign because of ill health. Bill is a retired local government worker and trade union official. He's Scottish, and also very good at writing and putting up notices, the latest being a warning to everyone about the dangers of using poisonous sprays on allotments. Not only are they antisocial, but they can spread to, and damage, other people's plots.

Apart from the ritual of autumn digging ready for the fallow winter, and the spring digging over the same ground to bring it back to life, the need to dig continues even into the summer. Right now, if I want to plant carrot seeds, or seed for a salad crop, I have to redig and smooth out a small patch at a time. Looking at the Croatians' wonderful plot by the gate, it is obvious their approach is much more organised. Everything looks so neat, and is flourishing. But there are sometimes up to three of them working intensively on their plot. Since my wife no longer helps me, or seldom comes to our plots, it is quite a struggle.

Am I becoming one of those men who uses his allotment to get away from his wife? I don't think so. Although at times I enjoy the solitude, there is always Joe, Jerome, John Johnson, or Angelo who come and go, and provide company if needed. I always tell people that half the time is spent talking, rather than gardening. It depends purely on how you feel on the day.

There are some days when I will attack a job, or others when I will sit in my shed, sift through the seed packets, or browse through a cookery or gardening book. I keep several books in my shed for this purpose. I have a paperback on growing vegetables by Lawrence D Hills, on the shelf at the back of the shed. I store newspaper to light bonfires, but we rarely have bonfires these days, preferring to compost most of the waste. But there will be at least one bonfire to light to get rid of all the bindweed, which is the bane of my gardening life. No matter how clean the ground is, bindweed will return somewhere, although I find digging a patch and removing it quite therapeutic, as you discover and pull out great long white roots of the stuff and put it in your weeding bucket. If you just leave it on the ground to die, it will reawaken and grow down into the soil again. The use of rotavators for ploughing up land cuts the bindweed into many fragments, which regrow stronger and more thickly across the plot.

Although nowadays I light a bonfire very rarely because of my belief in composting all the waste that I can, the newspapers I have stored can come in handy on very hot days when I wrap a cold French beer in newspaper to keep it cool. There was a period when I used to dig open a bean trench in the winter and put newspapers at the bottom, to hold the moisture. I would then empty our kitchen waste into the trench. There was a fashion to do this up until about five years ago. When I first had an allotment that is what all the old boys advised, if you wanted to be rewarded with a good runner bean crop.

Real composting has taken over fortunately, and the kitchen waste and precious golden human liquid is put to a use that improves the whole plot. The runner bean crop certainly has not been affected by not following the trench preparation programme anymore. So I keep filling my five compost boxes. I have cut all the comfrey down and put it in them, as well as some of the giant horseradish leaves and nettles. More grass has come over the fence from the Scottish brothers. My horseradish plot always causes me a problem, because I cannot get rid of it. I dig a root up and it just regrows. I was left with it from a previous plot holder. Its roots make excellent horseradish sauce. I either add it to a powerful commercial ready-made variety, or just grate it and add crÈme fraiche or yoghurt.

Across the plots everyone's thoughts are turning to holidays ahead. I haven't been away for three years, and if the weather is warm I am loath to leave the allotment during the crescendo of its crop-producing period. Juliet and Gemma seem to have no plans to go. I did phone my friend Rob and enquire whether he was going to Cuba again. Then we both think we might go to France for a week or so. I love France, not only because of the wine and food, but because I can buy exciting French seeds there.

John Johnson is slightly taken aback because Giuseppe has asked him if he would keep an eye on his plot while he is away . . .for three months. Giuseppe is on his plot today, and keeps it very neat. Today he has his two grandchildren and his wife with him.

Both children are intent on watering, and, like all young people, love sloshing the water around in each other's direction on purpose. They are allegedly helping Giuseppe plant runner beans, which will no doubt all be ready at the same time when he is away. John Johnson is very tolerant, but it is a bit of an ordeal with the plot owner being away for so long. Maybe it will rain for most of the summer and save him a lot of trouble.

*   *   *

Giuseppe uses an interesting technique on his artichokes. He places white plastic cups over them when they start growing and the effect is to produce closely bunched small fruits. When he talks about them it is like the chef taking over from the gardener, as he enlarges on a mouth-watering recipe. After boiling the small artichoke for a short period, he mixes together cheese, garlic and olive oil and pours this over the artichoke just before serving. He is scornful of just using vinaigrette when eating artichoke.

I scurry away and place a plastic cup on the

only artichoke that is small enough for this special treatment. But I know I won't have the confidence to carry out the whole treatment and recipe. Juliet likes the artichokes harvested for the home when they are not worth eating and burst into a bright blue flower, which looks beautiful.

It is now early June and, after a period of watering, there is a welcome brush of rain. Nothing like it for making crops grow. You can water and water but the hard London version, dosed with fluoride, does little but keep things alive. It certainly does not seem to make anything grow.

I decided to do a bit of clearing up next to the main bean trench which I have started planting. I now plant what I call the short side, adding some of the bright pink beans given to me recently. I dig the path clear, with my raggle-taggle raspberry patch next to it. At least I will be able to stand on level land as I reach in and seek out berries. There is still more bindweed to be dug out of this side of the bean trench.

Strangely it is quite cold today and a stop off for tea in Joe's shed is really needed to warm up. It is one of those days that when you are working you are quite warm, but when you stop you cool down alarmingly, and need to put another top on immediately. And this is meant to be summer! I have been telling people on the allotments that we would get a very hot summer, because we always do when the Australian cricket team tour here. I'm afraid my know-all sporting information is proving rather inaccurate at the moment. Almost as inaccurate these days as the BBC weather forecasts.

We are joined in the hut today by Steve and John Roberts. Steve's shirt is open and sleeves rolled up. John says that he should put a top on as it is too cold today to risk a chill. Steve reasons as to why he is stripped down like this on a chilly summer's day. 'I'm not a gardener. I was brought up on a farm looking after the horses. Then when I came to England I was a scaffolder for thirty years, and worked stripped to the waist even in mid-winter.'

When we finish tea he takes me to his plot to show me how advanced his tomatoes are: dark green, standing up tall and strong, and almost bearing friut.

John has something else to worry about in the poly-tunnel, where it seems a new inhabitant is causing chaos. It is a rat. It is particularly partial to John's current pride and joy, the boxes of corn. The best box, all ready to sell with an order for the following Sunday has been killed off completely by the wretched rat eating the corn seed beneath the plants. So John is putting the rest of the boxes into his car to keep at home, until they are fully grown and he can bring them back on a Sunday to sell.

There is a discussion about how to rid ourselves of the rat. Someone, somewhere, has a bit of rat poison in his shed. There is a trap, which was used earlier when rats were bothering Benito's chickens. When the offending rat was caught it was still alive so Angelo dunked the trap into a water tank, and that was a swift end for the rodent.

We set a trap and put the poison out. John did not tempt fate by bringing his lovingly grown corn back. After all there were no less than seven boxes of it still safe, and orders galore. Soon afterwards half a rat was found in the pile of manure that had recently been delivered.

When we find a good skip you can spend half a day lugging stuff out of it, loading it up on our big flat trolley, then pulling it slowly back to the site. That is what Joe and I were doing on a dull summer Saturday morning. Is the weather really being changed by global warming, or were the summers of our youth always lovely? I have no doubt something dodgy is going on, because the seasons have shifted, and there does not seem to be as much rain as there was.

Joe and I lug huge pieces of treated timber out of a skip we have found. They have come out of a roof the builders are dismantling to replace with a loft conversion. There are also a couple of pallets that he has kindly left especially for us on the side of the skip. For me there are several thinner strips of wood that will make good stakes later for the tomato crop, and anything else that needs support. Why go to a garden centre? I buy bamboo canes from our shop, which are eight feet tall and work out at a little over £3 for ten; certainly enough to make two small wigwams for beans, or one big one, which Joe has made and looks very efficient. I also use them to train the beans up on my smaller bean trench, which is under an elderly pear tree producing large fruit that seems to rot on creation. John Johnson is keen to remove this pear tree because it looks as if it is about to crash down onto his netting cage. We both agree to wait until the end of the growing season, so that he can fell it across my plot.

I will then plant another tree in its place, because I feel we should have a tree-planting plan as part of our future. Another of John Johnson's endless skills is his pruning and lopping of trees. This gives more light beneath them, as in the case of the massive yew that towers over one end of one of my plots, and over two of his sheds. He has also been assiduously removing the ivy that has twined itself round several trees over the years and threatens to kill them. He amazes us by perching precariously up various trees, as he saws and cuts. But it is now paying off as two of our older and most valuable trees have never looked in better health. A tree specialist at Kew Gardens once came round our site and said that two of our trees were very old, and valuable environmentally, and are on the protected list, so can't be removed. Nature even has its own defences against developers!

One of the sites that we lost to the Park Club had been used to film a TV series about a detective, Maisy Raine, who had an allotment that she used to escape from all the pressures of her job. The lead actress was Pauline Quirke, who had become famous for playing Sharon in the hit TV series *Birds of a Feather*. She was a very pleasant person and, like all women who come into contact with him, took a great liking to Joe, who helped the director in making sure that everything was accurate in the filming. It amused him that they brought in their own vegetables, slightly out of season, and 'planted' them in the soil, to make it look more like the public's idea of a real allotment.

Joe's shed at the time was a bigger version of the one he now has, because he had to move plots when the axe fell. However, it became the centre for tea-making and anything else the cast required. We would sit in there and chat to anyone who came in. It was an interesting experience, and there was great excitement among us all when the series was shown and Maisie used to go up to her allotment. She wasn't there very often, yet despite her absence it looked quite neat. Well gardened, Joe!

On our plot one of our new members, Charles, who works for the BBC in management, has started to build a shed, guided by John Johnson, and as a result one end of his plot looks like a builder's yard. At least the pallets and timbers Joe and I rescued from the skip will be of use to Charles.

John is measuring up, so it will be a good job in the end, but it may take some time to complete. It is quite ambitious with a glass window Charles has brought from home. The miracles of recycling. I go on and on at home, much to my wife and daughter's boredom, about the need to recycle. Yet how much is being wasted, especially good wood, in our consumer-driven society, and it is the poor countries, who cut down their trees to provide our wasteful needs, who suffer.

Bill Geddes has his plot next door to Charles, so I dropped in for a chat. Bill had a very constructive idea to waken up those who are not looking after their plots. He will send them a friendly letter, rather than a formal warning. He feels that he might lure them back to their plot, or they might choose to leave altogether. There are one or two plots on our site that have not been well tended, or hardly tended all season. Bill has taken a walk around the Vale with Joe and found one or two others suffering from, hopefully, temporary neglect.

The result is astonishing. People we have not seen for some time start reappearing. They have all sorts of excuses, of course, and none of them relevant. Joe is especially annoyed by one woman who returns to do a minimum amount of work and accuses him of giving her one of the worst pieces of land on the site, which is why she has had difficulties. In fact it used to be the best half of the first plot I ever had. I remember that only half of it had been dug, and it was the end she now had. The other half was barren.

Now we will have to wait until the end of the season before we repossess it. We could do it sooner under our rules of non-cultivation, but it's so far into the growing season that we will just have to wait until the rents are due at the end of October, and she can be struck off our list. Dan, the archaeologist, who unselfishly gave it up because he felt a whole allotment was too much, would now willingly take it back as he has cracked the whole gardening thing. His crops are growing really well and providing him with what he needs, but now he has discovered the knack of it all he feels, quite rightly, that he could expand. He does a lot of work for the Channel 4 series *Timewatch*, and has just been away in Ireland, where he got very excited about finding extremely old human remains in a bog. It was constantly having to travel with the *Timewatch* team that made him give up half of the plot.

He has done so well with the half that was left that the other half will be restored to him for the following season, no doubt. He is one of our younger members, and Joe, John and I are always reminding each other of the passing of the years, and the need to get younger members really involved in the site, so that they can take over from us.

The sowing season is now in full swing in order to get a succession of crops. One drawback of an allotment is that everything comes at once. No matter how you stagger the sowing of various seeds, they all seem to be ready to harvest at the same time. I am not having the greatest luck with carrots, for some reason. Either it rains heavily the day after I have planted them and the tiny seeds presumably get washed away, or the land is so dry and I miss a day's watering that they do not seem to germinate.

I love fresh carrots, and would love to grow row after row of them throughout the season—but I certainly use enough packets of seeds. Maybe I should sieve the soil before I put them in. I have a sieve, which I never use, but it would guarantee the tiny carrot seeds had smooth soil to flourish in. John Johnson is continuing his experiment by first planting a box of carrots in his greenhouse and then planting them out, just as I have done with my parsnips. However, he reports that the first batch he transplanted have tops but no carrot beneath, and that as far as he is concerned the experiment has failed. Unfortunately I won't know for several months if my own parsnip experiment is a success or not. At present they have good tops and they have all rooted, and I keep them regularly watered. I wonder if there is anything growing beneath these lovely dark green tops? It would be no good pulling one out to see, because they have months to fill out beneath the ground yet.

I have come across a new seed catalogue, quite late in the season, and cannot resist sending away for some seed. It is Chiltern Seeds based in Ulverston, Cumbria. The pictures in the catalogue are so beautiful that they are offered as prints, and they use original Latin names for their plant seeds throughout. I just have to buy some of their annual chrysanthemums after reading the personal way in which they write about all their seeds: 'This is the popular (well, actually it deserves to be more popular than it is) and easily grown annual chrysanthemum. Ideal for the children's garden, ideal for grown-ups. Long-stemmed flowers—smashing for cutting—in lots of different colours. A sow-and-forget plant.'

For once this is just how it has turned out. Brilliant. Lots of differently coloured flowers. I was cutting them for Juliet, but she said I should keep them on the allotment. I grew them first in boxes at home, and she has planted some out in the back garden flowerbed.

At the back of the catalogue they have a much smaller vegetable section. I buy some of their French thyme. This grows very well, and has a good smell and flavour. I also succumb to their French climbing beans, because I'd mislaid those given to me by Debra. They promise a violet flower, and dark, almost black, pods. Mmm. I'm not sure about that. I add some cucumber Bedford Ridge, and carrots for good measure, as well as some other flowers and chives. It is a lot more expensive than Tuckers, and I feel slightly guilty. Anyway the catalogue is a good read, and in future I will probably just buy their flower seed.

I have also been reading a book by W H Hudson, first published in 1898 called *Birds In London*. My version, bought from the Chiswick Community School car boot sale for 50p, was published in 1924 and underlines what Joe and I have experienced about the wretched robins this past spring. Hudson notes how fierce they are despite their 'sweet exterior'. I wish I had read this before all the robins' nastiness started.

I prefer the timid thrush and the opera singer of a blackbird who are accompanying me on my plot at the moment. There are plenty of colourful finches too, high up in the elder tree next to my shed. The finches are a bit rascally as they are likely to feed off the buds on fruit bushes and trees, causing havoc if they remove too many. The elder tree has two uses in the summer. First it produces lovely clumps of white flowers, from which Juliet makes a very tasty non-alcoholic cordial that can be diluted with water, and is an excellent thirst-quencher on a hot day. Then later on it produces black elderberries from which you can make elderberry wine, although I find these homemade wines too strong and high in alcohol. The only mixture I like is adding sloes to gin, which rather obviously makes sloe gin.

The elder tree towers up side of my shed, and the birds obviously like it as they remove all the berries. The birds will soon let you know when the fruit has ripened, because they will be in there either removing the whole piece of fruit or pecking a large gash in it. I will have to watch my grapes this summer, because the plant given to me by Peter Springall, who has allotments on the slopes below Crystal Palace, is really taking hold, and will produce a lot more bunches of grapes this year.

Fortunately, grapes do not need much water, because their roots go down several feet and find the water table quite easily in London. They don't seem to want feeding either, although I might put some of my first home-made compost on them at the end of the summer. Angelo shows me his dessert grapes, which are for eating, not for making wine. Mine are, coming from the great winemaker himself Peter Springall. Angelo says that Italians who make their own wine in London wait until Italian grapes are brought into the wholesale markets and buy them in bulk. I give Peter a phone call to arrange to visit him in the autumn on his site at Sydenham, or when he is picking his grapes. He tells me enthusiastically that a new allotment holder from Turkey has gone into the vineyard side of things in a big way, and planted rows and rows of new vines, which look really good. He urges me to go over there and see for myself. He is very pleased that someone else is taking on the mantle of winemaker, as he is now in his eightieth year.

My grapes won't mind but there has been a distinct lack of water all year. There is always the threat of a hosepipe ban. This is already being operated by Southern Water in Kent and Sussex, where the reservoirs have dropped to low levels, and small rivers are drying up altogether. It is in this area of Kent in the South East that the wretched John Prescott would like to build thousands of houses. The locals wonder where all the water is going to come from to keep all the new homes and infrastructure supplied. In London, Thames Water have come in for heavy criticism from the water regulator, because of the number of leaks in their pipes causing massive waste and loss of what will become a worldwide precious natural resource.

John Johnson has some good news for me. He has found me a rake at a car boot sale for a mere £1. He is an aficionado of car boot sales, travelling far and wide, especially down to Kent where one of his favourites is held at Brands Hatch every Sunday. I'd mentioned that I was looking for a rake, and he took on the job of finding one. I am partial to car boot sales myself, although our local one in Bromyard Avenue, where all the locals meet, was closed when Virgin bought the ground from the council. When I am not rowing, I go on the first Sunday of the month to the car boot sale at the Chiswick Community School, where I buy plants. But they do not seem to have many tools anymore. The trouble with car boot sales these days is that they have been taken over by dealers, who bring trucks of goods, rather than old books and tools the ordinary person wants to dispose of. Chiswick is good in that it serves a fairly wealthy area, and what the wealthy see as rubbish, the rest of us see as bargains!

John Johnson has found me this excellent all-metal rake. So I ask him to keep a lookout for a tool used a lot by the Europeans on our sites. It is a large hoe-like implement, almost like the smooth side of a pickaxe. The Italians, especially, use it to break up their soil, and almost dig with it. John says he will do what he can.

He arrives nearly every evening now, as the evenings lengthen, and it is light until well past nine o'clock. He puts on his carpenter's apron and sets about making something or other, having set himself up a workbench. The plants in his greenhouse are growing well, especially the tomatoes. He gives me four spare ones; neither of us knows what sort they are but I plant them beneath my old plum tree, which this year seems to be diseased. It is a Victoria plum, and they are very nervous, if you can use that word for a plant or tree. Some years they will produce an abundance of plums, and then the next hardly anything at all. You can never tell what is going to happen with a Victoria plum.

As far as I am concerned I can never have too many tomatoes. They have so many uses, and nothing can beat a home-grown tomato sliced, salted and with a little olive oil drizzled over it to accompany a good piece of cheddar. Imagine my horror, therefore, to read in Simon Hopkinson's beautiful book *Roast Chicken and Other Stories*, this dismissal of the home-grown English tomato: 'I don't think that home-grown tomatoes, even in summer, are that good.' This interesting cookery book has suddenly come back into print, because it has been voted by leading chefs and cookery writers in a Waitrose magazine poll to be their favourite.

After he gave me the gift of the four tomato plants John went back into his long greenhouse-cum-growing shed and handed me a large round radish, which he had grown in a box. It was wonderfully hot and spicy. My own radishes have been an absolute failure so far this summer. I do not know why, because I keep them well watered. I don't think anything can beat a good shower of rain, but how does that explain the excellent John Johnson radishes grown indoors?

So paranoid do we all become about the lack of rain that when it happens it tends to wake you up as it did me this morning at 6.15 a.m. But it only lasted for half an hour and I wondered whether it had rained at the allotments. Fortunately, it had when I arrived there to plant four cucumbers that I had nurtured at home. I put them over by the stinging nettles that I allegedly keep for the butterflies. This is true, but I should compost more of them. They are next to the never diminishing field of horseradish. I also plant some more beans in the main trench.

Joe and I are entertained at lunchtime tea break by Pat, who is a seamstress and has just finished working on *Strictly Dance Fever* for the BBC. She had a daughter at Gemma's school, and made all the clothes for the school play, an expert the school was very lucky to be able to call upon. She has the plot right in front of Joe's shed, which she gets various Irish relatives to help with from time to time, although it is very much her plot, and when she is there she works very hard. It is hard to believe she has finished a job making dresses that took most of the night to complete. Each competitor has to have a different outfit for each routine.

*   *   *

Pat jokes about other fellow Irish on the site saying that Steve had taken to his bed for a week after losing all his potatoes. However, in reality I do not think he has. But he may have another plot somewhere else that I do not know about, where he lost a crop.

Pat bought quite a few fruit trees last season, and they seem to be flourishing. Steve uses a bit of the ground by Joe's shed for himself, where he grows some cabbage, cauliflower and broccoli.

It seems to me that the summer is still sorting itself out; the weather cannot make its mind up what to do. Nothing seems constant about this summer and for me it has yet to be a good growing season. The potatoes carry on growing beneath the ground, but with hardly any rain so far they may not be that good. Listening to his radio Joe tells me: 'It was on Irish radio today to spray potatoes against blight.'

When I came back from my lunchtime tea with Joe there was a new tool leaning against my shed, delivered by John Johnson. It was just what I'd asked him to find for me. As I was putting it carefully into my shed he appeared and said: 'I've got bad news for you. It cost £4.' It was in perfect condition. Cheap at the price I felt! John Johnson had been on his car boot sale travels again. I used it for the rest of the afternoon, as I prepared the slightly dampened earth for sowing.

Charles's shed-building continues apace, with John Johnson keeping an expert eye on things. Weather-wise, this is the first really good weekend of the summer, and despite early drizzle, it has really brought a big turnout to the plots this afternoon, with plenty of children, and our wonderful new plot holder, a woman in full Muslim dress, working busily away. For me this is what it is all about. Everyone enjoying themselves, and getting some work done.

As I return to dig, Juliet arrives and sets about picking half a plastic carrier bag of gooseberries. It was Juliet who always did the planting, and I did the digging, but these days she is too busy running her literary agency, as well as the house and driving Gemma, now seventeen, here, there, and everywhere. I miss working with her up here. Two pairs of hands always made the work easier. I plant a row of spinach, two rows of carrots, and more lettuce, even though my Webb's Wonders are now strengthening and growing into something looking like real lettuces.

Lastly, hoping that the rain that was forecast might come during the night, I plant out twelve broccoli plants I have grown at home. I have dug a square almost under the yew tree, in the theory that it sheds all its greenery in the winter, so there is plenty of light. Since John Johnson has trimmed it back there has been more light anyway. I put wire guards over them, because the pigeons who live higher up in the yew tree would soon be down and peck them to bits. It is strange that they don't peck at the weeds. Quite often birds peck at plants just to get some moisture.

Birds, and their doings, seem to be dominating our lives recently, what with the robins, the diva-like blackbird and now a young woodpecker that has been rescued from the road, where it crash-landed, probably on its maiden flight. It was very lucky not to have been run over. However, it was brought in and given to Paola, who has put it in Benito's glasshouse. He used to keep some chickens in there during the winter, before he got too many and now they have a fine reconstructed home outdoors.

Paola opens the door carefully and points to a dark corner. When my eyes become accustomed to the lack of light I can see a small bird, with its claws stuck around an upright piece of wood, just as fully grown woodpeckers do when they cling on to the trunk of a tree. It is a sweet little bird who already has a red flash of feathers on its head, and black and white baby feathers on the rest of its body. It is obviously very frightened, having been nearly killed and parted from its parents. Paola says that she is going to put it in a cage for the night, in case a rat should come into the glasshouse. She gathers some small insects and a few grains of the corn she feeds to the chickens, and shuts it away in another darkened shed, so that it will be safe and relaxed. Its future is questionable. It will hardly be reunited with its parents. We think it must have come from a nest in a nearby park, and will have to be released.

The next day Paola reports that she was up early and let the young bird fly away. It took off well and flew, fortunately, inwards over green land, with no more trying to use the road as a runway. So all might be well in the long run. We can but hope.

With the summer season now in full swing several little niggles between plot holders begin to surface, which have to be dealt with by John Roberts, Joe, Bill Geddes and me as the dreaded committee. There is always the perennial width of paths to be addressed, as everyone tries to scrape an extra inch of land for themselves, with the result you can hardly wheel a barrow down some of the side paths.

The main path linking the whole site has just received a new coating of wood chippings courtesy of a group of young people looked after by the Prince's Trust, who had to complete several tasks before receiving their award. We had been asked if we could use such a group. At first we thought it might be a good idea for some energetic young people to dig out the road leading from the main gate to the shop, so that we could fill it in with all the rubble and bricks we have been given from the builder, who is working on the old vicarage next door. But when we had our first meeting with their leader, and the young people themselves, we realised that these are inner-city kids who would not be up to this very physical job. There is also the modern worry about health and safety, and we would not want anyone to injure themselves, so we decide that wheeling barrows of the lightweight wood chippings up to the end of the long path that links the whole site, and working back towards the shop, would be ideal for everybody. It would employ different young people doing different tasks, such as filling, wheeling and emptying the barrows, and then raking the chippings level back along the path. It would also benefit everybody on the site. So that is what happened. John Roberts helped run it and went to the awards ceremony that was held in a room at nearby

Queens Park Rangers football club. He was impressed by the young people at the event, and their work was certainly beneficial to us.

The minor niggling continues in the background once the path project is over. We have split several of our plots in two, and this has proved both popular and successful, although it has also brought its own problems. There are arguments over where the boundary line should be, but we leave that to our one-man United Nations representative, Joe. He has a long measuring tape, and uses it to solve all disputes. There can be no argument with Joe's tape measure.

There are complaints that the prickles from something growing on the border of their neighbour's plot is affecting and scratching them. Other problems are caused by thoughtlessness, such as a metal stake protruding onto a path at eye level, nearly removing someone's eye. When I went to investigate this complaint I tripped, ironically, over a metal object jutting out from another plot at ground level.

Someone else accused a neighbour of using a 'spray', which has affected their onions and garlic. We take a look at this alleged infringement and find nothing except that the garlic was starting to dry off and turn brown as it ripened. Our chairman Bill Geddes has already put up a notice warning people about the indiscriminate use of weedkilling sprays, and how it can not only affect your own plot but your neighbour's as well, if the wind is blowing in the wrong direction. There are one or two light brown telltale signs that it has been used on grass paths and also on some plots. Our view is that you cannot control where all this poison ends up. It doesn't just stay on the grassy path, which should be cut and not killed anyway, but seeps down into the earth on both sides, thus affecting the next door plot.

I return to the wildness of my own plot, which I love, because I could be in the middle of the country here, not a quarter of a mile from the A40. I stumble over something that is not a matter for the committee. It isn't a protruding piece of metal, but a hedgehog. How he or she had got here I do not know. But they are of great use to gardeners, because they live mainly off slugs. So the hedgehog is welcomed as the subject of many allotment conversations on how to rid our plots of these crop-destroying pests that seem to be getting larger. When I was a little boy in Sussex, we had quite a few friendly hedgehogs, which we used to feed on a daily saucer of bread and milk. So the next day I did bring a saucer and some milk. He hadn't wandered far, and seemed to enjoy what I had brought him, lapping it up very delicately. It was a good sign that he was here, and proof that the sprayers of poisons were in the minority.

However, as suddenly as he had appeared, he was gone, having one last drink of milk before taking his leave.

After her experience with the baby woodpecker Paola can now be seen walking her pet hen up and down Benito's plot as she works. But she is worried about it and is considering taking it to the vet, as she thinks it has something stuck in its craw. I said that I thought an Acton vet might be taken aback when somebody produced a hen out of a basket, instead of a cat or dog. It does still peck away at the ground which is a good sign, and she has given it some sort of medicine. The trouble is that Benito originally got these hens from Southall market and there is no hint as to how old they are. They probably came out of a dreadful battery after they had served their purpose. Paola's hen might just be reaching the end of its lifespan.

'You could always eat it,' I teased, bringing forth a shriek of, 'Of course I wouldn't.'

I remember when another Italian, Mario, was alive. He had one of Benito's hens to eat, and gave Joe a piece of it, and Joe said that it was very tough indeed. I think you really need to know the age of these hens. I gather they live for about seven years.

We are all interested in when Adis is going to get his hens. Adis was born in Fiji, studied in Australia, where he fell in love with Volkswagen cars after driving one across the

Nullarbor desert. He came to London and first of all worked in a large west London garage that specialised in Volkswagens before setting up his own repair business. He can, as a result, construct anything. In readiness for his hens he has built a virtual palace and we reckon the work has been going on for two years. In fact Joe has become quite caustic about the whole process. The arrival of Adis's hens has become a running subject of conversation.

The great thing about Benito and Paola's birds is that they lay quite a few eggs, and if I meet Paola at the right moment when she arrives in the morning, she gives me some fresh eggs. They make wonderful omelettes, and are even better soft-boiled. The yolks are a wonderful golden colour, and are even fresher than so-called free-range eggs.

The potatoes are beginning to grow well now, with some recent, and welcome, rain bringing them on. The only trouble with rain is that it encourages the weeds as well, so I spend the first part of this afternoon weeding between my Cherie potatoes. I have been lazy, I'm afraid, because I have not earthed them up properly. This is one of the processes of growing potatoes. Once you have planted them in rows you draw the earth up each side, leaving a trench between the rows. The idea is to cover the tops of the potatoes in the early days so that they will not get stunted by any frost. If the weather is dry you water the trenches so that the moisture goes down into the roots of the potatoes. I realise what a difference it would have made, as I compare the rather poor results of this whole bed with my well-earthed-up Romano and Fir Apple patch. As a result they look much healthier, which is a pity because Cherie are my favourite after Charlottes, which I so stupidly forgot to order.

So I weed away, but it is getting warmer and after yesterday's exertions of coxing at Dorney Lake, near Windsor, I think I will have a sleep, hidden away here in the innermost part of my plot, behind the main bean trench. I get my rucksack from the shed to use as a pillow and the DAF towel to lie down on, which I got all those years ago when they were the first sponsors of Sir Steve Redgrave. I still remember him getting it for me saying 'You've got to have one of these'. For some reason we had met that day at the Thame Show, the biggest one-day agricultural show in Britain, It must have had some sort of sporting value in those days, but it has ended up in my allotment shed, not wanted at home.

When I woke over an hour later, with a slightly burning face, I decided to walk over and see whether Charles had finally finished his shed, which was taking on hotel proportions, not in size but in usefulness. Suddenly there on the path ahead of me was a bird, best described as a smaller version of a rook. It kept on hopping along the path in front of me. At first I thought it might have an injured wing or leg, but as far as I could make out it was all right, although it did stagger first this way, and then the other, then it would regain its equilibrium and continue along the path as if it were my guide.

The bird continued to run along in front of me right up to where Charles was finishing off his shed. He was quite impressed by it, and we both agreed that it had obviously left its nest too early, and had not yet learned how to fly. How nature puts some of its produce at risk, with the marauding foxes, and the reappearance of a cat or two. We have been missing cats for a year or more, and blamed the foxes. Now that Somerfield has closed down, the foxes do not get their evening meal from Stewart the Scotsman anymore, so they seem to have moved on.

Stewart is normally to be found in the afternoon sitting outside his little green hut, which is on the main path as you go by the shop, listening to the radio, reading the paper and sipping at a can of lager. He has his hair swept back in a ponytail and a well-weathered face. He speaks of going to business school at one time in his past, and running a pub. With him often is Jonjo who has just turned eighty. He comes from Galway, and rides an old bike, which has a mind of its own. One day Juliet

94

and I were returning from Chiswick when a cyclist shot across the road in front of us. It was Jonjo. It was as if his bike were bolting with him.

Today's hot mid-afternoon sunshine then gives way to a cool evening. Just the conditions for the dreaded tomato blight. John Johnson with his superbly built long greenhouse to protect many of his plants will benefit from all these varying conditions.

At least I have given him one piece of successful advice. He was going to remove the raspberries from under the big yew tree we share because of the shade. He followed my advice and just pruned them almost to the ground and they are booming. If only I could take my own advice!

The recent rain has speeded up my flower planting in the bed in front of my shed, which I now like to have almost wholly given over to flowers, some that I can cut for the home, and the rest to be enjoyed here. Elsewhere I plant carrots, lettuce and radish seed, but I fear the worst, because either it pours just after they have been planted, thus washing them away, or it is so cold they just stay, quite wisely, beneath the soil. It is amazing how plants do this. They will hang around for ages unseen, and then just when you think you have lost them a few warm days will bring little green shoots through the earth proving that they are in fact alive and growing.

One day in Morrisons, looking at the seed display, I cannot stop myself buying chives and lavender seed. I am going to grow both of them in boxes indoors. I have grown a small lavender bush near the front of my shed from a cutting I took from somebody else's lavender on the allotments, and at home in the tiny back garden we have at least one small bush. But I want to rival the Slovenian woman next door who has a whole row of this beautiful lavender, which attracts the bees, and has a wonderful refreshing scent when brushed against with your hand.

As the evenings stretch out Stewart and Jonjo can be seen sitting outside Stewart's shed drinking lager or wine. The more they drink the louder they become. I ask Joe what they talk about and he replies with a touch of his Irish irony, 'Mainly about what they are going to do with their plots.' In other words they sit longer than they work. But why not? I know exactly how they feel, and if I had that time on my hands I would no doubt slip into that lifestyle myself.

Jonjo always has a word for me when I arrive and pass by their shed with my bag of kitchen waste and in the other bag, carefully hidden through my own embarrassment, the golden liquid. 'Here comes the farmer,' Jonjo will say with Irish enthusiasm. On another occasion this will be changed to 'the late shift is arriving.' He will usually have a remark too about the state of his potato crop. As he has yet to harvest it, I am not quite sure why he is already complaining about our buying policy, saying we are not buying the right seed potatoes. It could be that Joe is often teasing him, and drawing him into all sorts of false beliefs. For a man of his age, Jonjo is remarkable: actively digging, cycling and with a full head of unruly white hair and usually wearing an old jumper even on the warmer days, with his trusty bike parked right next to him.

The first plot I pass, apart from when I first come in the gate, is the one in front of the shop belonging to Maureen and her partner David Bays. They are avid organic gardeners and help run the West London Organic Gardener. Their plot is always admired. Not very large, compared with some, but always producing fruit or vegetables. They have recently introduced a small plastic greenhouse, in which they are growing herbs like basil. You can see a hint of the real organic gardeners that they are; next to their beans there are grapefruit halves placed open-end down on the soil. I presume this to be some sort of slug trap. I remember years ago the mighty Lawrence D Hills showing me how he put fat on a string beneath his fruit bushes so that the birds would come and not only peck at the fat, but also any nasty little insects that would attack the fruit.

The next plots are Jonjo and Stewart's, and then after Charlie Rycroft's large compost bins you come to Pat's plot, which is in front of Joe's shed. Next door to that is Joe's tool shed, where every tool you would ever wish to use can be found. Joe's sight is no longer what it was, but he can still remember where he put every screw and nail when you want it. Tool sheds like these do not happen overnight, they represent a lifetime of allotment work. Collecting all the time, and thinking of the future, and what might be needed—never throwing anything away. The BBC girls also keep their tools here for the while.

Whether it is the influence of the Prue Leith cookery course or not but I seem to be harvesting a lot of rosemary this summer. It is around most of the year, and I am always nipping bits off the top shoots to poke into the ground, in the hope they will grow. Sometimes they do, sometimes they don't. But I have got quite a few new small bushes in the making. For some reason there comes a moment in the life of a rosemary bush when it just gives up, its wood becomes brittle and it dies off, so I just keep on planting a succession of tiny shoots. I use fresh rosemary to chop up finely, mix with olive oil and press into Stewart Taylor's first Kent lamb of the season. I buy from Stewart weekly at the Thursday morning Hammersmith farmers' market.

The first flowers of the summer are ready. I

cut dark red Sweet William flowers, which seem to have remained in the ground, where I never expected them to be. I was also able to take home a large bunch of long-stemmed daisies. They have to be cut down every autumn, so that they thrive the next year.

I put wire protection across the strawberry bed: strawberries which John Johnson dug out and gave me in the autumn. However, although the wire prevents attacks by birds from above, it does not stop the slugs appearing from beneath and emptying out the middle of the fruit. I should have put straw or wood chippings around the whole lot. I think I got a little too confident, and now I have been punished. All around me people seem to be picking large quantities of strawberries; it is better for me to keep quiet and eat the few that have survived right here on the plot.

The good thing is that the strawberry bed has grown and there is obviously a future for it. I might even extend it. Debra has given me a block of alpine strawberries which I will plant under my plum tree, because it is too early to add them to the strawberry bed while it is producing. When they produce runners later on, I can either bury them and they will produce new plants right there, or snip them off and produce my own plants in a box

Debra's greenhouse is busy producing at the moment; she has box after box of lettuces, cabbages, basil and peppers, and is always offering me something or other, such as the alpine strawberries. In return, and often unknown to her, I pop into her greenhouse and water the plants if they look a bit dry after a hot day. The great danger about things being grown indoors is to not water them enough. I know that at home in my conservatory, the seedlings need a heavy drenching morning and evening as soon as it gets warm.

One Sunday morning I walk over to the Chiswick Horticultural Society's shop, just opposite where the monthly car boot sale is held. I cut through the grounds of Chiswick House, where the precursor to the Royal Horticultural Society was housed in the 1800s when the Duke of Devonshire owned the property. It was originally built in the two years from 1727 by the Duke of Burlington and his protégé William Kent who was everything from artist to landscape gardener.

The gardens are being gradually restored, and it is hard to believe that, when the Duke of Devonshire was there, he filled them with kangaroos, which were prone to attacking visitors, a multitude of goats and an elephant. The great Joseph Paxton started work there for the Horticultural Society. Paxton later became the nation's leading gardener working with the Duke of Devonshire at Chatsworth, and also designed the great glass exhibition hall for the Great Exhibition in Hyde Park, during Victoria's reign as well as the original Crystal Palace, which lasted eighty-two years until it was burned down in 1936.

The shop at the Chiswick Horticultural Society, run by Geoff, was as busy as ever, putting our own into the shadows. They have 600 plots, or more, and, six helpers in quite a large permanent building, which opens on a Saturday and Sunday. They also have another shed given over to storing compost and other bulky things. You can buy anything here, and after being offered a piece of home-made cake and a coffee I spend £1.20 on half a dozen allotment-grown eggs. The seller has forty hens and, therefore, quite an output. Today there is also a pile of second-hand gardening books on sale, as well as the plants outside that Geoff buys at dawn at the Columbia Street market in the East End.

Geoff and I swap notes about what is selling in our particular shops, and what is not, and then he switches the subject to what is happening to the Green Party's London allotment initiative, a much-needed London association of allotments to cross-fertilise information. We both agreed nothing much would probably ever happen. I told him about the much more promising meeting at Walthamstow Town Hall with local authority allotment representatives. Geoff would like to be involved in this, and should be. What both of us wanted was a cross-London organisation of the different associations to swap information, such as where to buy things at their cheapest; share bulk deliveries to cut costs; and to be able to summon instant support if any of us were threatened by developers.

I told Geoff how well our polytunnel is doing and he laughed and said we were copying him. I wasn't aware they had a polytunnel. He is the perfect person to have in charge of an allotment association, because of his energy and ideas. He staged their own show last year at the old Chiswick Town Hall. Debra entered and won one or two prizes, Typical Debra. She has so much energy . . .I just don't know where she finds it! This year Geoff hired a marquee and put their show on Chiswick Green, but that proved a little too expensive. I like the restlessness he has brought to his society. You never know in which direction he will lead them next.

Unfortunately the Green Party initiative is just another talking shop—a home for moaners and ranters—instead of being positive and forward thinking. It would be far better to set up a forum for local authority officials, who actually deal with allotments, and could meet two or three times a year. Neither of our own local authorities (Hounslow or Hammersmith and Fulham) attended the meeting at Walthamstow Town Hall. Hounslow has outsourced the running of its allotments, and there's no representation from the profit-conscious company that runs them. I urge Geoff to progress towards self-management. His members support his plans and offer their spare time to work in the shop and on the show, which is a better response than we have ever had.

The strong point about the local authorities coming together as an allotment forum is that it is run by Ealing's Stephen Cole, the best person that has happened to allotments in London for ages. As for the cross-London association I suggest to Geoff that we build on what we have in west London: exchanging thoughts, prices and ideas. The way we run our association is in a rather relaxed manner. We do not call official committee meetings, but John Roberts, Joe Hughes, and I are in constant contact, and can call upon our chairman Bill Geddes, who is usually there on his plot.

After walking back through the grounds of Chiswick House I decide to attack the horseradish square, trying to curb its acceleration. I put some of the giant leaves into one of the compost boxes, because Alf Barnes, our organic gardening expert, says that they are a very good ingredient with which to make good compost. As they grow it looks as if it is one more piece of ground that I am not cultivating, but I cannot do anything to stem them. I do dig out the small ones every year, in an effort to make the patch smaller but this is one battle with nature I will never win, unless I get a mechanical digger and set about removing the whole lot.

I did see a chef on television recommending making horseradish ice cream. Not too much of the horseradish, of course, but just enough to give the ice cream a bite. I'm afraid even in my wilder moments of cooking I am not going to follow this recipe. Although it is said that strawberries taste better for having a little ground black pepper on them. Something else I have not hurried to try.

Being self-employed and working at home is difficult when it is a beautiful summer day like today. This is the best day of summer so far, and the plot calls. I can hear the blackbirds from here, tempting me. I gather up a bag of kitchen waste, a full six-pinter of the golden liquid, and slip quietly out of the house, with a feeling of guilt, but also of delight as I plan what I am going to do. For a start there is a bit of land to be dug halfway down from the overhanging yew tree. Then I will put up a couple of wigwams made from the bamboo canes and sow some beans. Wigwams seem much more productive, and maybe this is the beginning of the end of the traditional runner bean frame. Joe has constructed a slightly elongated version, but we both agree it works better than the frame, maybe because more air and light is available as the sun moves around during the day, and the wind blows around it.

For the first time I water with the hose, which has been overgrown by a combination of nettles, weeds and comfrey. I thought someone had taken it, which is often the way on an allotment. Something goes missing and you think immediately that it has been taken by someone, whereas in fact you put it down somewhere, turn to do other jobs and forget where you put it. So it had been with the hose, given to me last autumn by Adis.

This stolen time is going to be put to planting for the future; I put up the wigwams, and reach to tie them together at the top. Unlike Joe I have built one quite tight one, putting the poles very close together so that they take up very little space, and one of normal sized circle. The beans I have put in are a mixture of the French climbing beans, and the heritage beans from the HDRA.Then I plant a couple of rows of spring onions, some radish and spring cabbage, and lastly some mixed lettuce leaves. There is already some lettuce I can pick, and also some yellow and white flowers to take home. Finally I cut a couple of sweet peas, to add to the ones I have already taken home. Their smell is delicate and rewarding. It has been well worth sneaking away from my desk. This is one of those moments when I realise how important the allotment is in my life. Away from it all, away from the inner city, which is still all around us, but not visible from certain points of the plot. The blackbird is back in full voice, and the thrush scuttles across the newly dug soil.

Back at my desk I get a call from a newspaper enquiring whether anyone is growing cannabis on our site. It is a question that comes up from time to time, gardening as we do within the inner city. Some people may be looking to cut out their dealer and get it direct from the grower. This time I trace the rumour back to a storyline on *Coronation Street*, where it is being grown on an allotment.

I tell Joe that I've had this enquiry, and say I suppose we could grow it in the polytunnel, because of its heat and light, which are the two necessities of cannabis production. Years ago during my days involved in the rock world there was a regular supply from a flat in a council tower block in Plumstead in the East End of London. It was good quality, and there was plenty of it until the grower was arrested, but he had to keep the lights and electric fires on twenty-four hours a day. I had to tell the newspaper that it was almost impossible to grow cannabis outdoors in Britain unless there was a very hot summer. There was a fashion at one time to plant it in the middle of a farmer's wheat crop so it was hidden from prying eyes. But I never got to smoke the results.

Joe said that one of our plot holders from the Far East recalled that cannabis grew wild in their country, in the same way that that in the Irish countryside there was a good supply of wild garlic growing in the hedgerows. Joe then told me a story he'd heard recently. An agricultural tale of a very unpleasant goat, even by goat standards. It refused to be milked, or have its hair combed to sell. So the farmer decided it would have to go. He knew no one locally would buy it, because everyone knew of its reputation. So one day he announced that it would have to be killed. One of his farm boys heard his decision and begged with him to let him have the goat, thus sparing its life. Eventually the farmer agreed and the boy took the goat home. As he had no land of his own he tethered the goat daily around the district. After a while the farmer made a visit to the boy's home and asked to see how the goat was getting on. Imagine his surprise when the boy led out a now docile goat, who was quite happy to be milked in public, and then have her hair combed. The reason for this great change in character, it turned out, was that the goat had been feasting daily on large amounts of wild cannabis!

Joe reflected on the story he had just related and pondered on whether this treatment would stop some of the current warring on our site. We certainly wish calm to return, but we have no wild cannabis to provide the remedy.

I've got the garlic, but it isn't wild, and I must say this year's crop is some of the best I've ever grown, but unfortunately I've forgotten where I sourced each of the two different sections that I have grown. Typical. Too much ad hoc gardening going on here. When will I get organised, and record everything from seed to harvest?

This week's brief burst of real summer also brought our Slovenian family out for lunch, on their little patch of lawn next to their neat shed, which houses their table and chairs.

The lawn caused some controversy when it first appeared. Several older male members complained to me about the grass and said it should not be allowed. I had a quiet word with our Slovenian friends and asked them if they could plant a herb bed within the lawn and the furore died down. Allotments seem to attract officials who like to add their own rules to the book, so that the rule book becomes so large you can hardly do anything legal on your plot at all. In Fulham there are what we all look upon as the posh Bishop's Park site, the pride and joy of Hammersmith and Fulham council who hardly provide any allotments in their borough at all. But Bishop's Park has a rule for every day of the year as far as I can make out. You aren't even permitted to grow fruit bushes, or fruit trees. They would certainly not allow a part of an allotment to be set down as a lawn. But as the Slovenian family have a delightful two-year-old, Nicholas, who now possesses his own little spade, I allowed it. After all, allotments are there to be enjoyed, not to reflect the past allotment age of Arthur, a former plot holder in *EastEnders*.

Another complaint put to me was that there were too many flowers being grown. Some allotment-society rules forbid the growing of flowers, saying that vegetables are the real reason for allotment gardening. When I the analysed the complaint I realised that I was the one growing the most flowers, because I like to cut them and take them home. They are more mixed, and unusual, than anything you would get in florists.

My favourites are the dark blue cornflowers, most of which I leave growing for the bees, and to enjoy their dark blue colour from my seat looking out of my shed. I grow them from seed indoors in March and transplant when the conditions outside have recovered from the winter. Similarly, I plant a box or two of multi-coloured statice, which, when flowering, can be used immediately indoors, where it will last almost for ever, or, as is more usual, cut and dried for colour indoors through the winter.

Despite loving sweet peas, I'm not very good at growing them. They can be started off at home but are so hardy they can be planted in a box outside the kitchen door to be transplanted later, but mine don't seem to flourish. I had even sent for some sweet pea seeds from Sarah Raven, the rather expensive entrepreneur. The result was not very good! And the same could be said for her lettuce seeds as far as I was concerned, but it could well be my fault. I admit to having a rather cavalier, farming approach to allotment gardening.

I am not alone in my somewhat ad hoc approach. Some years ago we had a plot holder who had spent his life serving in the army. As a result he could not sow anything in the straight lines he had been forced to stand in all his career, so anything he grew shot off at tangents all over the place.

A significant moment arrives when, for the first time, I open the bottom door of one of my compost bins, and start to cut away at its contents It is truly rewarding, a horticultural equivalent of chocolate cake, as it comes out in slices to be put in one of my big plastic buckets and carried across the plot. I am putting it on the site that I have earmarked for the planting of my leeks, when, and if, the rains come again.

It leaves a hole in the bottom of the bin, and I suppose in the end the rest will just fall down upon it. I don't know how much of the waste has been turned into compost, but this is a very good beginning, and there are lots of small red worms working away for me. At last something I have done on my plot has succeeded. Meanwhile, I confess, I watered some of the burgeoning crops with a can of Miracle-Gro, which I have favoured for the past few years, although we do sell a seaweed extract in the shop. Perhaps I will try it on some of the other things such as courgettes and cucumbers when they are near fruiting and need a bit of a boost.

The arrival of my first home-made compost is very fulfilling. If I can add some more boxes to my already growing collection I might be able to become totally self-sufficient, and never need even a spoonful of Growmore again! My own brand is certainly solid and moist, like good fruit cake. Although I use the hose to water the main beds again, I still find myself reverting to the watering can through choice. I like to deliver a drink personally to each of my plants, especially the flowers, so that I know how each one is progressing, despite it being time-consuming.

When I go for tea with Joe he tells me he is having trouble from the robins again. He thinks they are having a second brood and, therefore, returning to their bellicose behaviour. I hope not, but fear the worst when one of them bumps my head on purpose as it flutters up to the nest above me. The robin wars are obviously being renewed.

The warnings keep appearing on radio and

television from Thames Water that as there is no rain, and as the heat increases, there will soon have to be a hosepipe ban. The weather has been so hot that the plants wilt in the daytime and when arriving in the evening at the plot, at first glance it looks as if everything has died. This week the water company has been heavily criticised by Ofwat, the body controlling the now privatised water companies, yet again for not mending as many of their leaking pipes as they should. When it does rain they have a nasty habit of emptying raw sewage into the Thames, which is causing illness among some local rowers. The hosepipe ban would save us money, as in the hot weather many plot holders leave a hose running to water in between their rows of potatoes. For the first summer ever I am watering with a hose, which is in full use every night, and I'm feverishly—literally in this heat—picking lettuce every night because I have a steer at Henley Royal Regatta. For rowers Henley is the Royal Ascot of eights racing. I am to move clubs and steer Kingston, which will mean travelling down there on the tube and bus most evenings. I'll have to come up here first thing in the morning or at lunchtimes, which will stop me eating. Hence the mad rush for lettuce, as I have to drop my weight quickly to the race weight minimum of 8 stone 9 lbs. In fact you need to be 1lb or more below that so everything is under control, and you know exactly what you can and cannot eat. This hot weather is perfect for not eating.

The tayberries have also ripened now and I'm able to pick them every day. The big group of Webb's Wonders are keeping up the lettuce supply, along with some mixed leaf lettuce I planted among the flowers on the land in front of my shed. When the really hot weather comes it is time to plant French beans, because they love warm soil and grow very quickly. You can put them in earlier in the year and they won't show at all. French beans are definitely warm weather seeds.

We move into Henley week and the weather immediately cools down. I soon find that there are secret allotment holders everywhere. One of the Kingston coaches, Mike Clarke, tells me that he has an allotment, and that one day his wife said she wanted to buy him something special for his birthday. He joked that what he needed most of all for his allotment was a load of manure. Early on the morning of the great birthday he was awoken by the sound of a large lorry. It was loaded with horse manure, which it proceeded to dump near their front door. His wife had taken him literally, and organised a special delivery. Even though he had to barrow it to his plot, he was delighted. At last, he said, someone had given him something he really wanted. He talked to me as much about the growing of asparagus as

113

rowing. I knew exactly how he felt.

There was an almost daily shower of rain leading up to Wednesday's opening day of the regatta, which brought the broad bean crop on perfectly. They are always best eaten when small and tender; they are as good eaten raw at this stage, which some people prefer. They still need a regular wash from the watering can with a squirt of washing-up liquid in the water to keep the black fly at bay. My efforts to plant marigolds within the rows of broad beans to keep the black fly away, as recommended in many organic gardening books, has not worked.

The weather has really turned cold. I arrived back on the plot to find Les and his tiny dog. He is a great man for rumours, and says that there have been complaints about a woman sunbathing topless in the recent heatwave, but no one could prove anything. The other rumour is that Adis wants someone else to take over the plot next to him, in order to stop rows with his current neighbours. I check this with Adis, but say we cannot swap plots at this stage of the summer. Rumours once spread the word that the whole site was to be sold! This was said to be based on a chat with the owner of a house overlooking the allotments, who was selling up because he didn't want to become part of a housing estate.

As to the topless woman complaint, the next day Joe goes into more detail. It was Alf

Barnes who first complained saying: 'It's not a beach, it's an allotment.' Joe knows who the woman was and says that if it had been him he would have drawn up a chair next to her. We agree there is nothing wrong as long as sunbathing is discreet. When Carol and Jerome arrive that afternoon, they say they had heard the story and, looking at me stripped to the waist, mockingly jest that they should complain about topless men wandering about all over the place.

In fact, as soon as Henley had finished, the weather had suddenly turned warmer and I was digging stripped to the waist as I prepared a bed for my leeks, which I've grown in a tray. They are getting a bit big, but have good dark green tops. However, I will wait until rain is forecast before I put them in. First comes the hard work of digging a bed for them, removing the wretched bindweed, spreading my own compost across it. At the moment it is just there in a pile. As I am digging, Angelo looks at the bed being prepared and suggests that I grow some endive. I find it too bitter, but he explains that you can boil it, drain it, put some olive oil and chopped garlic on it and it is delicious. However, this stretch of land next to my parsnip experiment is to be dedicated to leeks, not endive.

Angelo continues to talk to me about cooking. He thinks it admirable that I should learn to cook properly. I intend to start in the autumn, part-time at Thames Valley University in Ealing, which runs chefs' courses backed by the London Tourist Board.

The Italians tend to drift between their allotments talking to each other in Italian, and they all know each other very well. Angelo tells me about Benito, who was a chef all his life. 'He comes from a tiny village near Bari that produces top chefs. One became chef to President Clinton during his period in the White House. Benito started work in the village at the age of twelve by washing plates, before learning every job in the kitchen. Eventually in London he became chef to the French Ambassador.' Angelo says that although Benito is now retired he still does the odd day for the German Ambassador, when his permanent chef is on a day off.

I continue to dig the patch ready for the leeks, spreading two buckets of my own compost across it when I finish it after two hours' solid work, with the sweat dripping off me. I am beginning to feel a bit stiff, no doubt because this is not the digging season. But I have to get this bit of land ready for the leeks, and hope that it will rain just before they are due to be planted. Meanwhile, Joe has three rows of leeks in perfect lines because he uses a string line between two stakes of wood stretched across the earth before he is about to plant. It is something every good gardener does, especially the older ones. I should do it, but can't be bothered. Hence my lines are never completely straight. I won't be able to plant the leeks for some time as the weather forecast continually talks about the hot weather persisting. No mention of rain.

The Mayor of London himself, Ken Livingstone, has joined in the cries for a hosepipe ban, because he says water is getting really short in the capital, and he suggests for good measure that we don't flush the lavatory when we have a pee. I feel like emailing him with my secret of the golden liquid and its properties, and how you don't need to use the lavatory to get rid of it at all. So there you are Mr Mayor, come on board, for water-saving organic compost.

Suddenly everything changes, even on the allotments. July 7th, and fifty-seven people are killed by suicide bombers on the London tube and a bus: a further 700 people are injured. Birdsong is replaced by the wailing sirens of police cars. The hunt is on for further would-be terrorists and there are several suspects in west London. All the local roads are gridlocked because of the closure of main roads in and out of London. It is a strange feeling being here among the greenery in what is usually a peaceful setting. Those sirens don't stop, and now there are police helicopters hovering over Shepherd's Bush.

The summer heat continues, and as Kingston decide to compete in the National

Championships in Nottingham I spend the Saturday morning coxing them up past Hampton Court, where the annual flower show is being staged. There are specially built pontoons, so that people can travel by river to the great gardening event. When I get back Jerome is running the shop, with John busy selling corn and other plants from the polytunnel. Jerome says that Hampton Court is a much better event than the Chelsea Flower Show, because it is not so snobby and you can buy things there every day. He remembers, however, going there two years ago when there were gale-force winds, unlike today's sullen heat. After he and Carol had been in one marquee everyone was asked to clear the area, because of the danger that the gales might damage it. When they got home they switched on the TV news only to see the same marquee they had been in that morning taking off into the sky!

Phyllis has brought some really useful cuttings from her home in large pots. They will grow even bigger, and fill the hole in the hedge made by a car on Benito and Paola's plot. Evidently it came around the corner too fast, and the young driver lost control, swerved across the pavement and removed part of our hedge. Fortunately no one was hurt, but it has left a large hole and Joe has put up a strong piece of wire fencing. Phyllis's hedge cuttings will solve the problem permanently when they are planted in the autumn.

Phyllis has been a member for years. Her husband Arthur died some years ago and she found the allotment was getting too much for her. Fortunately she has decided to return and John Roberts has found her a small plot on the Bromyard site near to his own. She has always helped out in the shop, and grown things in her own greenhouse at home to sell for charity. We are glad to have her back.

Jerome reports that the shop has taken between thirty to forty pounds during the morning, but we wouldn't expect to sell much at this time of year, although the polytunnel makes up for it. However, he did report that a lot of people turned up just for a talk, which is a good sign, and something we are trying to encourage. Hence the reappearance of Phyllis. We wish more members who have given up their plots would turn up on Sundays for a chat with old friends.

My job for today is to fix up a small cage to protect my broccoli, which has grown a bit too big for the wire covering that I put over them when I brought them up as seedlings from home. The pigeons have been at work on them, pecking through the wire and removing most of the upper leaves. A reminder that nothing is really safe up here from these marauders. Just as you think you have got away with it, they will remove all your greens

119

overnight, especially in this hot weather when they also get moisture from the plants they eat.

From somewhere I do find some energy and purpose, and set about digging out more of the patch by the broccoli that has already been planted, because I have some different sorts of broccoli brought from home to plant. Debra has also given me six Savoy cabbages that will go into the new square. I stamp on some of my curved metal plant protectors to flatten them out with the idea of making the new taller sides of a cage out of them. It doesn't work. I will need taller stakes, which I can then connect up with the netting I have found around my plot. John Johnson has been keeping an eye on me, and, realising that I am not doing this very efficiently, lends me a heavy hammer, and then breaks the stakes off exactly where I need them, with a quick snap over his knee. Gradually the covered anti-pigeon area is enlarged. And I put some of my compost among the new greens to help them on their way, and give all the plants a good dowsing of water, which causes a spray of white fly to rise like dust into the air, before they settle back on the broccoli below them. The next time I will have to wash all the plants with washing-up liquid in the watering can.

Washing-up liquid is an excellent mixture with which to defeat white fly, which home in on any winter greens and many other plants. It is cheap to use. A couple of squirts of the cheapest supermarket brand into the watering can, and you have a mixture that if used two days running will remove all the aphids that the ladybirds cannot find and eat, which I am afraid are a multitude. My first plans don't work, and eventually I have to bow to John Johnson's superior planning knowledge, and everything starts to fit together, as I salvage the now flattened metal guards. Once it is all erected, and obviously going to be a success, I know I will have to extend it to house more of my greens.

Back at home the phone rings and it is the driver of the lorry bringing us three sheds from just outside Reading, for which we got a local grant. All three, it has been decided, will go to women members, especially Kathryn and Jayne. The driver says that he is just outside Slough but does not know how to find us. He is half an hour away, he says. I find that rather optimistic as the traffic seems to get slower and slower in and out of London. I have to rush up to the site to see that the main gates are unlocked in readiness for his arrival.

I am right about the time of the lorry's arrival, and both Joe and Charlie are on the site. Why is it that whoever organises deliveries never rings up the day before to warn us, as we always ask them to do? It is a continual nightmare of our existence that lorries arrive out of the blue, and it is sheer luck if the site is open. As I repeatedly explain to delivery companies: we do not employ full-time workers.

Tonight is the night of the Eve Lady Balfour memorial lecture organised by the Soil Association at the Royal Geographical Society, and the main speaker is Dr Tewolde Berhan, head of the environment agency in Ethiopia. It is twenty years since their famine caused the giant Live Aid rock concert. Imagine my joy when Dr Berhan made the theme of his talk the use of compost, and how he'd taught the farmers, especially in the northern region of Ethiopia, to compost their weeds and animal manure. The result was that even though there was still a lack of rain, plants were growing where they did not before, because they were able to go deeper into the compost-filled soil which held any moisture there was. He showed large before and after photographs to illustrate dramatically what effect the use of compost had had upon farming.

Apart from this message he attacked the multi-national agribusiness companies for trying to introduce western methods into his country's farming and ruining the soil in their non-stop search for the quick fix with nitrates and sprays. He was also vehemently against the use of GM seeds.

*   *   *

The next day I took the kitchen waste and golden liquid to my compost boxes with a new spring in my step. At least I now know, from a real authority, that I am feeding my soil properly.

At the lecture I sat next to the chief gardener of the Henry Doubleday Research Association's organic gardens at Yalding, near Maidstone in Kent. He had held various good jobs at a Cambridge college where 'the soil was wonderful to work, seven hundred years old'. He moved on to Hever Castle, before his present post. I told him that the only chemical I now used was Miracle-Gro, to feed my tomatoes and other plants. He advised doing away with it, and putting some comfrey in the water butt.

It is the Saturday of the National Rowing Championships in Nottingham, and I have planned to be at the allotments really early, because it is going to be a very hot weekend in London but, fortunately for my Kingston rowers, not in Nottingham. It was 7 a.m. when I arrived, and already the side gate was unlocked. I immediately feared that someone had left it unlocked from the previous night, something that has been happening lately. This is not a good idea as crops come to fruition and temptation spreads for passers-by. But I need not have worried, because there was Danny Gallen, wheeling barrows of manure, and digging his potatoes. As I'll be away for two days I need to really hose the water on heavily, while the day is still comparatively cool. This is the ideal time to be up and about in London, because no one else ever is at weekends.

There is, however, a huge shrieking and bawling going on at the far side of the plot. It could be a fox killing a bird. A mass of feathers can often be found on a path, a sign that the foxes have been at work on the pigeons. Alternatively, this caterwauling could just be two foxes fighting, or even mating, although it seems a bit late in the year for that. I'd brought with me a huge dripping bag of kitchen waste, which goes straight into one of my compost bins. I fix the hose on the tap and water for half an hour. Then it is time to go. I have really enjoyed what is undoubtedly the best time of the day. No wonder Debra is up here so early. In fact I think this morning she has even beaten Danny and me to it. She must have arrived about 6 a.m. because when I look into her greenhouse to see if it needs watering, it has already been done.

As we come in to the harvesting season I am hit by a crisis that had actually been planned. Can you plan a crisis? The complete demolition of our kitchen linked with the installation of a major course of anti-damp work, and then the installation of a whole new kitchen was agreed in January. The idea, my wife tells me, is that if the work is done in high summer we can live outside on the patio on barbecues. The weather turns for the worse, which forces me to Argos to buy a Russell Hobbs classic kitchen. This is the modern equivalent of the Baby Belling from my bedsit days. You can roast a small chicken in it, and boil vegetables on its two top hobs. The drawback is that you cannot have the oven on at the same time as the large hob, and so you can't roast a tray of courgettes at the same time as anything else in the oven, because there is no room. This comes precisely at the moment that the courgette crop bursts into edibility. Plus my own garlic is better than ever this year, and ready to be sprinkled across the courgettes. Unfortunately courgettes do not take long to swell into marrow size if there is as much rain as is now forecast. A programme on LBC said that new kitchens are a frequent cause of marital breakdown, and now I understand why!

It is very hot and, having taken my weight down to 8 stone 8 lbs, I'm not that hungry anymore. We'd been knocked out of the National Championships in Nottingham by Saturday night, so the next day I was back on the plot worn out. I laid a towel out and used my rucksack as a pillow to go to sleep, hidden from the more active.

Before I went to sleep I had tea with John and Joe. Jonjo and Stewart are busy sipping cooling drinks. John says it is so hot the shop took only twenty pounds that morning. He has some growing advice for me about beans. If they are planted now they will grow and last well into the autumn, so I take his advice and put a handful along my sweet pea frame. They are Bunyon's Best, which I bought last year from the HDRA Heritage Seed Scheme in Ryton.

When I woke up from my afternoon sleep I picked a box of mixed fruit that the heat had encouraged in the past few days including tayberries, gooseberries, blackcurrants and raspberries. The courgettes had also responded to a mixture of my watering and the warmth, so I pick the two largest; one has a very dark, green skin, the other much lighter, almost yellow-striped. I won't be able to eat them but I will give them to Saul and Richard, who are working on demolishing and then rebuilding our kitchen. Before leaving I water inside Debra's greenhouse which is very hot indeed. She has a lot of thirsty cabbage plants growing in there.

Another Thursday, and another bomb in London. But this one, which didn't go off, was much closer, just down the road at the Shepherd's Bush Metropolitan and City line station. As a result the Uxbridge Road has been closed from where I cross it on the way to the site, right down to the tube station. There is more traffic chaos, and the sound of wailing police sirens is greater than ever.

The heatwave goes on, and so most of my energy and time goes on watering with the hose. My lettuce has not really been good this summer. Maybe it is me, but there is no succession. The early lettuce was all right, but nothing seems to have grown since, so I am grateful to Adis who has a whole row of red frilly lettuce, which he says I can pick whenever I like. My own lettuce lasted for the dreaded bout of weight loss. Ironically, for the first time for years I have nothing to cox during this glorious weather, and will return to the river in the autumn, when no doubt it will be as cold and wet as usual.

Some good news for me was that I came across one brand new pallet and another half a pallet, which I drag up to Joe's table. I think with all the disruption that is going on local roads builders are giving the Bush a miss for a while, and, therefore, have left behind wood they might before have taken away. Joe will take them to bits, piece by piece, and construct something really useful from them in the future. On the way home I go through the Alexandra estate and see another skip, which is loaded with old bamboo canes. Good enough to serve a purpose for me. I just hope they will be there in the morning when I return.

With no rowing, which occupies both mornings every weekend almost year long now, I can relax and plan two days' work on my plots. First of all I renew acquaintance with the West Ealing farmers' market, and buy a home-made pork pie from Lincolnshire, which Joe and I enjoy so much. But when I arrive at Joe's shed, he is not there. I leave everything in my shed, and go back to the Alexandra estate and the skip I had seen the night before with a stack of bamboo canes in it. Fortunately they are still there so I stack up with at least twenty of them and take them back to my plot. A really good haul!

Joe's shed door is still closed so I continue with the big job I have planned for the day. At last, the great planting of my leeks, and the reason is the heavy rain forecast for later today and tomorrow. The moment has arrived, and I cut the luscious dark green tops in half so as to make them work and become stronger when I plant them out. I plant over one hundred of them, breaking for lunch in my own hut. After wandering down to talk with Charles, who is back from holiday, I tell him that the monsoons are coming, and it is a good day for planting.

Still no sign of Joe, so I cut the pie in half and eat my share, keeping the rest for him. Despite the promised rain, I fill with water the holes that I have prepared with my dibber, and drop each leek into its own hole. As usual it is a sporting event that seeps across the site this afternoon. It is the first Test match between England and Australia at Lords, and John, the prison officer, brings news that all is not going well for England, and we both look up at the sky and hope the predicted rain will come to the rescue of England's cricketers. John originated from Hampshire, and is a great supporter of the Saints, Southampton's football club. Whereas John Johnson's radio is normally tuned into Radio 4, Hampshire John, like myself, listens to Radio 5 Live if there is an afternoon of sport.

I soon have a use for the canes I had collected from the skip in the morning, because, as they start bearing fruit, the tomatoes obviously need staking. The weight of the new tomatoes is beginning to bend many of the plants down to the ground. After I had staked a few, Tony arrived from the Vale. He has been working in Henley for several weeks at the regatta, and then the arts festival. He says that Joe is now on his plot, so I take the half-pie over to him. I must have just missed him because he had gone off to collect a load of wood with a friend who had a van available for the morning. Now he retreated into his shed to make us mugs of tea and eat his pie. We notice that there is, for once, a friendly robin pecking at the crumbs Joe has thrown down for him outside his shed. Joe throws more crumbs out to be pecked up avariciously. The rain did not come in time for my leeks, or, indeed, England's cricketers.

But it did come the next day after I had collected a few more old bamboos from the nearby estate skip. Before it actually started raining Angelo came up and took me to his plot to show me his fig trees. I bought a small fig tree at the turn of the year, but his are magnificent, several feet tall, and already producing fruit. He explains how wonderful fresh figs are with prosciutto ham. He has fig trees at home, and also inside his netted area his grape-vine is already producing bunches of edible grapes.

As it starts to spit with rain I decide to leave, but not before talking to David Bays who has the allotment just by the shop. David is so thin you do feel that one day a big gust of wind will break him in half. He has been very good to me; because of him I was called to give evidence to the Greater London Authority's Open Space inquiry. This was an initiative by London's Mayor Ken Livingstone to find out how much green space there actually was in the capital, and to what use it was being put. I spoke up for the allotment movement. David was working at the GLA at the time.

He told me that *Jellied Eel*, the quarterly paper of the London Food Link, needs a replacement writer for Richard Wiltshire, who writes the short but witty allotment column. In fact, I had already talked to Richard on the phone this week, and he mentioned that I might make a good replacement for him. He felt he had done it for long enough and he was busier than usual. He told me to contact Ben Reynolds. I did this and was invited not only to write the column but to become a representative on the London Food Link, which meets during the year and is aiming to establish a local food network for London, promoting a sustainable local food economy, as well as advising local and regional authorities on local food projects. All admirable sentiments that I agree with, and believe that it is something the allotment movement should be involved in. After all, we are producers of local fresh food.

Now housebound by the rain I plant a couple of boxes of lettuce, because we are eating so much salad as a result of not having a kitchen. I also plant another box of chives. I really should transplant the two boxes of rather straggly chives I already have in the conservatory—I haven't, because they have kept up a regular supply to be cut up finely and used on potatoes. I ponder yet again on why, apart from the early success of my batch of Webb's Wonders, this summer all my planting of lettuce outdoors has come to just one successful crop. Not even later planting of the Webb's Wonders, which I am now buying in all their chunkiness from the West Ealing farmers' market on a Saturday morning. You won't find them in the supermarket, and yet a couple of them will, if kept in the fridge, last us for the whole week. But they are a lot larger and thicker than the ones that I grew. I order lettuce seed for our polytunnel from the farmers' wholesale list at Tuckers so there should be no difference

The success of the polytunnel, under the guidance of John Roberts, continues. My only input now is to water the plants. Everything looks healthy and there is a good sale for January King cabbage plants at 20p each, ready to be planted now and harvested in mid-winter, as well as cauliflowers, which have never grown well for me. Perhaps the ground here is too good for them. They would grow better in concrete, which is perhaps why they do so well in the rocky region of Brittany in France.

*　　　*　　　*

Angelo comes by as I am admiring how the rain has refreshed my leeks. He is still very much the quiet Italian, no matter how long he has been here. He looks at my rosemary cuttings from the unusual rosemary bush two plots along and thinks they are too small and will not grow. Well, we'll have to wait for the result. I'm usually quite lucky with getting rosemary to multiply. It is just that this particular bush seemed rather different, so I couldn't resist breaking a few sprigs off, removing their spines and pushing them into the earth beside the leek bed. Angelo proudly shows me a bag of the first potatoes he has dug this season, and they did look good. He also held up a yellow vegetable enthusing 'zucchini'.

Jerome and Carol come by wheeling their bicycles up the path. It makes me nostalgic for the days when my wife and daughter used to be here. I return to my shed to leaf through one or two of the gardening books I have bought at car boot sales over the year. I keep a few here, just in case knowledge is needed, which in my case is most of the time.

I go over to Jerome and Carol who, after a spell of hard work, are sitting down having a small snack. They offer me some pieces of apple, which are delicious, and they say they have bought them from their fruit man at the Notting Hill farmers' market. I thought the prices might be high there, as it is a rich and fashionable area of west London, but they report that that is not so. Certainly the fresh English country apple is a good advertisement for eating comparatively local produce. The farmers' market movement has not only been the saviour of many a farmer, nearly driven mad by the demands and poor returns of the supermarkets, but also of the consumer. I believe we can eat better than those living in the country, with the allotment and the farmers' markets. Many places, like Henley, have a farmers' market once a month but we have a plethora of them in west London. I go up to Borough Market, London's most important market, which is beside Southwark Cathedral, which takes place on a Friday and Saturday from noon.

Having discovered the huge advantage of our polytunnel I cannot wait to tell others about it. I was having a coffee with Larry Wright, the head of Hammersmith and Fulham's Youth Offending team, when the subject of gardening came up as something his young offenders could do by way of paying back their debt to society.

I had to remind him of the day when I was sitting in the Youth Court and we handed out the mandatory sentence for a first crime by a young person, who had pleaded guilty. This is what is called a Referral Order, where the young person and his parents have to go along and sign up for a regular series of meetings with local representatives, the Youth Offending team, and the police. This boy, having been told that we were going to give him a three month Referral Order asked plaintively, 'It don't mean gardening, do it?' We assured him that it did not, and he relaxed. This was the point I made to Larry Wright about young offenders' views of gardening.

However, I suggested to Larry that

gardening within a polytunnel might be the answer, as part of something different like a Supervision or Action Plan where the miscreants have to report to the Youth Offending team two or three times a week for a set period handed out by the court. The idea in all youth crime sentencing is to stop reoffending.

At least in the polytunnel the young people would be warm, they wouldn't get muddy, and once seeds had been planted they would grow quickly because of the heat generated by the special plastic covering. He agreed, but asked who would pay for it and whether our allotment association would do it. I could not agree to this, as we had no room on any of our sites for it. As we were based in the London Borough of Ealing, I thought the Borough of Hammersmith and Fulham should look after its own. However, as we were always getting calls from residents of that borough for an allotment we could kill two birds with one stone and open up a site in nearby Ravenscourt Park. This is a large well-kept and busy park, which already had provision for basketball, soccer, skateboarding, bowls, a thriving café, and a children's play area. I had already earmarked a site where allotments could quite comfortably fit and we could put the Youth Offending team's polytunnel right there. I had also noted on the Internet that Red Nose Day funds were available for just such a small-scale financial scheme.

Later I delivered a map and the reasons for the site to the Youth Offending team's office. I warned them that the Parks department would probably object as they were very prickly about the land they controlled being used for anything other than a park. Yet, as with the allotments world, so with the parks. Things will have to change. I believe small plots serving the community could be managed by the Acton Gardening Association for the local council. Self-management is government policy, and we could provide it. Bert Simpson, one of our senior members recalled that many years ago when an Acton authority actually controlled Acton, the Acton Gardening Association managed all the local council plots for that authority. When the London Borough of Ealing took over they said the arrangement would have to end as they wished to rule. So there was a precedent to our management proposal.

Will this polytunnel business never stop? I am just about to arrive at the plot when a car hoots and pulls up. It is Jim Wong, who was chairman of the Acton Vale Residents' Association, until he resigned recently because he is relocating. It was Jim's wisdom that guided the re-building of the estate's community centre and sports facility, in which we also involved ourselves, as the estate is immediately opposite our Vale site.

He had guided us in getting the grant for the three extra sheds, and the paint for repainting our shipping container shop and notice boards. I don't know how it arose in our conversation but the word 'polytunnel' crept in, and Jim thought it would be a very good idea to put one on the estate so that flowers and herbs could be grown by the residents, or for the residents, so that they could put them on their balconies. Another original idea. The world is full of them until you involve politicians. The trouble with all these ideas is that everyone wants everything done for nothing, while permanent officials and even councillors get paid for what they do. No wonder New Labour is so keen on community involvement and the voluntary sector! Who will see all these projects through? Many of us still have to earn a living.

It has been raining again, and now we wonder if summer will ever return. The weather, whatever it is, never satisfies everyone. We are no exception. When I arrive at the site there is a tremendous racket coming from the top of one of our tallest trees. It is a lone green cockatoo. Most unusual, because usually they move in groups. Later when I go down to look at John's reclaimed land at the other end of the site, there hooked onto an old piece of tree is a beautiful woodpecker, with a red feathered head. I remembered our baby woodpecker rescued from the road but I don't think he would have grown up so quickly. This bird was quite mature, and I stayed motionless and silent for several minutes as he pecked at his feathers to clean himself. He then treated me to a secret drilling of the wood, before he saw me out of the corner of an eye and took to the air and away he went.

John Roberts has really brought this piece of land back to life. Before it was just a large ditch with rubbish strewn across it, as well as a fallen tree here and there. Now it is covered in a green canopy of huge leaves hiding squash and pumpkins, rows of potatoes, and runner beans.

Adis has a week off, and says he is going to finish off building the emporium that will house his chickens. It has taken him two years but he promises a culmination of all his work by the end of the week. Joe remains his usual dry, sceptical self. Adis is adamant now that the arrival of the hens is imminent, which is why he has taken this time off. He is aiming to fetch them by the weekend. He also wants a rabbit, which he says will run with the hens, but Joe and I dissuade him from this idea.

Adis works on, and is building small wooden runways up to the sleeping accommodation at one end. There are slats every few inches that make it like a ladder, so that the hens can hook on with their claws and not fall off. They are certainly going to be living in luxury, with plenty of room for them to scratch and walk around at ground level. Adis also plans a walkway around their home at ground level for when he is there, so that they can find worms and all the other insects they like so much. I walk with him along the rest of his allotment, and it is flourishing with long rows of carrots and spinach. Excellent! We move on down the path to the plot taken over by an American, who against all odds brought it back from neglect. Unfortunately he has had to work in Singapore and elsewhere ever since, and so the weeds have come back, but it will not take him long to put it back to rights when he returns. Our warning to him before he left about the pigeons eating his cabbage plants if he did not net them have, unfortunately, proved all too true. Some of them have been reduced to tiny stalks, the rest have disappeared. Still, there is a flourishing row of lettuce, and a row of peppers is surviving well, as is his small row of beans.

Adis says that if only the American had told us he was going away someone could easily have kept the weeds down for him, but I do not think they could have kept the pigeons away. Shortly afterwards the American does return, and soon his plot is back in order. We have to be very careful in choosing who should have a plot, in case that person loses interest, or was just a dreamer anyway. We have at least three people at the moment who are wasting our limited space.

Suddenly there is nearly a whole day of rain and everything springs forward again, including the weeds. Nothing replaces rainwater, and I must remind myself to fit the water butt to my shed which I bought at cut price through the council. I already have a makeshift arrangement involving a large plastic barrel, but this larger and built-for-the-job barrel would do a better job. Also I must creosote the shed before the winter. I am becoming the ultimate prevaricator.

The great day dawns unbeknown to the rest of us: it is this August Saturday afternoon that Adis chooses to go and fetch the chickens from a farm just beyond Guildford. 'Come and look,' he says to me excitedly as I follow him up the path to the far edge of the plot where the chicken emporium has been built. And there they are, already scratching around and very much at home. Adis pointed to a collection of brown cardboard boxes of various shapes and sizes that he had used to transport them in his car. All the boxes had big holes punched in them so that there should be plenty of air available to their temporary inhabitants. There were fourteen chickens in total, all of them the same Rhode Island Red crosses with beautiful cream tail feathers. They were almost a year old and looked in extremely good health.

140

Adis had already joined them inside their new home and was pouring mixed grain into a long shallow trough for them. He had bought four sacks of this mixture from the farm, as well as a large water hopper, so that there would be water available all the time. It had to be filled only once a day, and let out the water into the circular drinking bowl as was needed.

Well, it had certainly been worth the two year wait for their arrival, because they were already amusing us, by flying halfway up the first staircase. Any worries that they would not reach the top roosting space were soon dispelled. They proved very adventurous, as well as inquisitive. So inquisitive in fact that within days of their arrival Adis had to wear rubber boots all the time he spent inside with his hens, because they insisted on pecking at the toes of his trainers, and had already partially destroyed one shoe.

The chickens have become the showpiece of the site. Everyone wants to come and admire them. There is something incredibly peaceful just sitting, or standing, outside the pen and watching them as they peck here and there at the ground, or fly up the stairs, or just perch on a piece of quite thick branch that Adis had constructed for just such a purpose.

They are always quietly clucking contentedly, and nearly always on the move.

141

When you first arrive they all move towards you in the belief that you are bringing them food. So many people are fascinated by them that I suggested to Adis he charge a viewing fee!

After only a few days in residence the hens produced their first eggs. There were only three, and they were quite small, but it was a start. A week later Adis beckoned me to his chickens again, and revealed he had just bought six more. He had set off that morning to buy some fish at the West Ealing farmers' market, but then on a whim had decided to drive to the farm beyond Guildford again and add to his collection. I can quite understand why, because there is plenty of room for the additional hens, and they are such pleasant creatures, as everyone who has been to visit them agrees.

I note how well made the door to the chicken cage is, and Adis reveals that 'it was the work of my chippie'. In other words John Johnson. Is there nothing this man cannot make?

The builder who is completing the massive house rebuilding next to Paola and Benito's plot has just delivered a lorry load of old-seasoned timbers that he has taken out of the old roof, and Joe has set up two wooden stools so that he can place them lengthwise and patiently take out all the nails. They will provide the base for several new sheds in the future, no doubt. The builder is also going to deliver a huge number of pallets, because a load of paving bricks is about to arrive. The pile of bricks he gave us when he was starting work nearly a year ago is still beside our entry road, awaiting our plan to make a hardcore surface. They have been there so long now that weeds have grown all over them. This is because we have decided the job is too big to dig by hand and it will need a machine to do it.

As I pass, Charles is busy scattering grit along a small trench he has scratched with his hoe prior to planting a row of carrot seeds. He says that the best carrots on the allotment are grown by Adis, who has two long rows of them, with healthy green tops, which no doubt his hens will enjoy eating while Adis and his family eat the carrots beneath.

Charles says that Adis has worked out after all these years that it is best to put some grit in with the earth, and that keeps away the slugs. I'm not so sure about this approach. I too have suffered, like Charles, from planting rows of carrots only for the odd one here and there to actually grow. But I think this is because this summer's rains have been fairly heavy and frequent, and usually just as I plant my seed. I'm convinced this washes them all away. I really don't think grit will make that much difference. However, you cannot argue with the splendid show of carrots that Adis has produced this summer.

It is strange working out how to grow something. It may all be on *Gardener's World* on TV, it may be in every gardening book you have on your bookshelf, yet in the end there is no explanation out here on the plot as to why a crop does not grow well. I do think that certain things grow well for certain people.

I discuss the failure of my lettuce crop with Joe, and tell him that we are buying two huge Webb's Wonder lettuces from the farmers market in West Ealing every week. I underline that they are, as usual, as big as cabbages and I cannot work out why. Joe thinks they grow them in polytunnels, so when I next visit West Ealing I put all these theories to the farmer who grows them. He said the answer was simple. 'Good old Lincolnshire soil. I grow them outdoors, and the soil is silt.' Simple answer! Our base is London clay, but I shall try with a large amount of compost to make conditions better for them. However, as the farmer added, short of borrowing a field from him, I wouldn't ever get as good Webb's Wonders as he produced.

I have not attended the Greater London Authorities Biodiversity Committee for a while, because I got disillusioned by the lack of feeling about the role allotments play in London's environmental life. I am encouraged to receive an email about a report they are bringing out and I reply that allotments

144

should be mentioned as part of green space in London. After all, that is how this committee began its work—as a result of the Open Space inquiry. I am delighted to get a reply from Dr Jan Hewlett that I have made a good point and she has passed it on to those compiling the final dossier.

Suddenly there is an important sighting that would add substance to future biodiversity discussions and links with allotments. John Johnson reports watching a stag beetle fly from the elder tree above my shed across to the yew tree above his shed. 'It was like watching a heavy bomber. It flew very slowly, it was quite large, and then it flew back again.' He also saw a stag beetle coming out of a crack in the tree next to his shed, but could not tell if it was the same one. He believes not, because the original beetle returned to the tree overlooking my hut.

Then out of the blue I get an email from the London Wildlife Trust inviting us to attend two Stag Beetle Conservation workshops. The first is in Richmond Park, the second in Bromley. They will deal with the life cycle of a stag beetle, how to provide stag beetles with a suitable environment, and status and threats to stag beetles in the UK, among many other aspects. It is signed by the Stag Beetle Officer for London Wildlife. Suddenly the presence of a stag beetle seems rather more important than it was before.

We are now in the full flow of the harvesting season. Every year, it seems that everything comes at once. Where is the hoped-for succession? Suddenly I have bowls of tomatoes at home, and I am giving many away to friends, and even fellow allotment holders whose crop has yet to arrive, or worse still has been destroyed by blight.

The spinach is in full cry, and, because of the loss of our kitchen, all my courgettes have turned into marrows. I have given many courgettes away, but not many people like marrows anymore. They still taste good with a cheese sauce, or stuffed with imaginatively spiced-up mince.

I am saving what carrots I have for better days. Now the beans of all sorts and sizes are arriving. The French climbing beans are a very colourful dark mauve, until you cook them and they turn green. Yet they have a better taste than the beans I have grown on the ground before. There are plenty of runner beans and some nice flat beans, which must have been produced by the bright pink seeds. You eat them just like runner beans sliced up, but they taste better.

At last we have our new kitchen and I use the French beans a lot as a curried vegetable to accompany the main meat curry. My potatoes are producing well, but I find that the Cheries don't lend themselves to currying as well as the hard new potatoes from the supermarkets, which is a pity. However, I do find I've a lot more Cherie than I thought I had planted. The Romano are good bog-standard potatoes for mashing or roasting, and I have the weirdly shaped Pink Fir Apple when I want a firm waxy potato for when we have a salad with the main dish.

Looking to the winter ahead the greens are growing well, now that they are protected against the ring doves and are watered regularly. The parsnip experiment looks well from above ground, but the tops may be all I get in the end: you never know what they will turn out to be down below.

Every year I look on the desk in front of me in my shed, and go through a few seed packets that I have kept apart from those that I have been using throughout the season. They are the over-wintering varieties of spring onion, and lettuce, as well as wild flowers to be planted in September. I can honestly say that I have always forgotten, or kept them too long past their planting time, in the past. This year I resolve to make a plan and stick to it.

Unfortunately, as the temperature rises outside, so does the dispute between Adis and one of the other plot holders. It is mainly territorial, as are most disputes when you get to the bottom of them. It is all very unfortunate because Adis does so much work for the Association, and I would be loath ever to get rid of him. Then there are the chickens that everyone loves, and are now laying on the hour every hour. I heard one celebrating the fact with a high-pitched contented clucking only a few moments ago. Unpleasant relationships between one plot holder and another are never nice. I have been through similar situations in the past, but found that the passing of time is the real healer.

To add to all of this there remain certain plots suffering from not being fully cultivated, and there has also been another rush of applicants lately, to whom I respond that we will not know until the end of October if we have any space for the coming year. I think our chairman Bill Geddes, who is now back from his three-week visit to the Celtic music festival in Brittany, will be having an inspection of all our sites with Joe, and then a few letters may be winging their way to wayward plot holders, who can be weeded out in the autumn.

It is the holiday period, and this will be the third year I have not been away. This is partly because of being at home to oversee the work on our demolished kitchen, and then the discovery that Juliet had forgotten to renew her passport. Our daughter Gemma is busy taking art courses at St Martin's and the Victoria and Albert Museum, so there is no opportunity to go away this year. This is also not the best time to go away if you have a working allotment, as you will miss out on the enjoyment of eating a lot of your crops.

Jerome and Carol are going to France for ten days and ask me to water their plot, mainly their corn on the cob, which is still growing. I don't mind this. In fact for the first few days it rained quite steadily so I didn't have to do anything. Then when it stopped I discovered what good gardeners they were. It was like having a practical lesson in how to run an allotment. They control, between them, two large plots, which used to be run by Dorothy and her mother, always known simply as Mrs Fuller. I presume this is the same plot that her mother had when she saw First World War Italian prisoners of war demolishing the local manor house.

Dorothy's husband, it is said, died after a session on their allotment, but she kept it on until four years ago when, overrun and in a totally unkempt state, she had to give it up through physical frailty. Bravely Jerome and Carol took all this land on. Of course, other people now want a part of it since it looks so good. But you have to remember how it was before they arrived.

I fastened their hose to the tap and started watering nightly and admiring especially the length of the stems of their sweet peas, which as their temporary gardener I was entitled to pick! My wife was delighted when I brought these beautiful long-stemmed and delicately scented multi-coloured flowers home nearly every night. I reckoned I was also doing them good by cutting them regularly, as well as watering them heavily. They produced bunch after bunch of flowers for us.

I watered the corn on the cob well, and their row or two of potatoes, which were still growing. They also had an open-sided greenhouse with climbing beans in it. I noticed they were the same flat variety as those from the bright pink seeds that I had been given. I held back on this part of the watering, because beans grow very quickly once they have taken hold. I didn't want the beans to be over by the time they got home.

They also had a whole bed of squash and other huge round marrows and courgettes, which they said I could help myself to. I ate the raspberries that were on the outside of their raspberry cage. They were all large, another thing my own fruit never aspired to. I do not know why. I came home nightly to Juliet and talked about how Jerome and Carol grew all these wonderful things in an orderly fashion. It drove me back to my own plot and some really hard work with the spade and a scythe to get it into some sort of order.

Sadly the best raspberries were in a cage that I could not work out how to enter, and had to watch them turn rotten before my very eyes. I did get plenty though from the plants outside the cage, which were protected from the birds by a huge piece of white material. A great deterrent, but not to a human who knew how tasty and large they would be once you had located them.

When they returned they were, fortunately, pleased with the results of my watering, and then I revealed to them how good I thought their sweet peas and raspberries were and why, and asked them how they achieved this. Carol said that the sweet peas were an old-fashioned mixture, hence the length of their stalks, and that she would buy me a packet of the seed. As for the raspberries, they both said that when they dug out some of the plants this autumn they would give me some. But will these things grow for me? I will have to change my approach. Maybe prepare the ground more carefully over winter with an ample supply of my own compost dug in. I will consult Carol again before I do anything. Obviously I must keep my ground cleaner. That is the real lesson.

*   *   *

Already I have started keeping my ground cleaner where I will put the raspberries, as the blackberry season, which came early this summer, is now over, and the wild blackberries I let grow are over. I will need the space if I am to emulate Jerome and Carol's raspberry crop, especially if they give me some of their canes. I will trail my thornless domestic blackberries that have been such a success at last, burying part of them beneath the soil. This is called 'layering', and hopefully the pieces below the earth will grow new roots and my original thornless blackberry will enlarge itself. I plan to give it its own piece of fencing to grow around. This summer it was confined to one end of the sweet pea frame.

Things are happening apace now in the reinvention of my plot. On John Johnson's plot are some new wooden uprights. Can he be building yet another shed? He explains that this will be a vertical part of his plot, with blackberries trailing up around the posts by wires, as well as fruit trees espaliered along wires. This means making them grow their branches neatly sideways, rather than anywhere they wish. He comes across and looks at my young trees to get an idea how he will do this. I have rung the fruit farm in the West Country to get a new list, but despite someone saying they would send it, they have not done it yet.

John Johnson, who seems never to cease in pushing his plot forward, has offered me three of his curved supports that have until now formed his outdoor frame protecting his greens, strawberries, and a few other things. They will cover ten feet of ground, and a width of ten feet six with a door. This, I have decided, will be the frame for my own polytunnel. I take the liberty of asking John if he will help me construct it because of my practical uselessness. He readily agrees. There is even a door at one end that comes with the tubular supports. All I have to do is to order the special polytunnel plastic. Excellent—I will be able to grow salads during the winter, if I hurry.

Just as I was basking in the warmth and harvest of this summer, the weather took a bit of a dip and there was a crisis. It was a Saturday morning, and quite cold. I had gone across to the nearby Homebase to buy some Roota in readiness for my autumn programme of propagation, encouraged by the book I bought at the car boot sale published in 1933! When I came back Charlie Rycroft and Adis were just leaving. It was only mid-morning, but not a very nice day to spend on the site. They mentioned that one of our members had apparently had a fit, and was lying down, resting, on the path, near to his shed. They asked me if I would check on him to see if he was all right when I left. As I did not intend to leave for most of the day I went back to my shed, and then thought I should have a look to see how the man was getting on. When I arrived he was lying prone outside his shed, looking unwell. Inevitably, I'd left my mobile phone at home, but as I walked back to my shed I saw Paola's white car arrive on the far side. I knew she always used a mobile so I went over and told her what had happened. She rang the ambulance service for me, and I spoke to them. They were very good, and within minutes an ambulance arrived. Paola was very supportive and had already had a look at our patient. I had to explain to the ambulance staff that typically our man was in the far corner of the site. The team were a man and a woman. The woman soon told us that she had just got an allotment near Northolt, and had had it for four months, and was finding it pretty hard work, because of the hours of her job with the ambulance service. I said that she was welcome to come to our shop any Sunday, and we would give her some good compost and plenty of help and advice.

As we got three-quarters of the way to where I'd left the prone body I looked up the long path and there was our patient walking towards us. I apologised to the ambulance people as the man explained that he was an epileptic, something he had suffered from for several years. He took tablets, but admitted that he had a fit maybe once a week, when he passed out.

The lesson from all this, as I said to Joe and John Roberts later, was that the committee should be informed of any medical condition any of our members suffered. We would then know what to do. The whole experience took a lot out of me, and I went home early.

Sadly the evenings are beginning to shorten,

just enough to remind us that summer is coming to an end. It is also quite cold in the evenings, even after a hot day. Autumn is beckoning, but the seasons do seem to be shifting, being wetter in the spring, and warmer during September and October. There are still late raspberries to eat; potatoes to harvest; Angelo's figs are fattening; John's reclaimed wilderness is producing a mountain of pumpkins; the tomatoes keep coming although blight has spread over part of the site.

The time has come to plan for next season, which promises to be better than ever. Maybe I should just remain at the planning stage and not garden at all. But that is the attraction of an allotment, you never quite know what will go right or wrong, and you'll always get plenty of advice, whichever way it goes.

Summer Recipe

French climbing beans. When they are just past their youth, which is the best time to eat them plain boiled, or even raw, I find currying them as a vegetable accompaniment to meat or chicken curry a family favourite. Much nicer than those neat little trimmed French beans from the supermarket. In a little oil melt one shallot, finely cut, grate an inch of fresh ginger, two chopped cloves of garlic and a teaspoon of mustard seed. Parboil beans, refresh under cold water to keep colour and put into a pan with the other ingredients. Simmer slowly, adding a teaspoon of crushed coriander seeds, cumin and a few curry leaves. Keep stirring, and test regularly for readiness.

Summer/Autumn

The first honorary secretary I can remember always appeared on the plot neatly dressed with a collar and tie. His shed was carpeted, and within it any small meal could be prepared on a gas ring. In fact, he breakfasted there at half past eight every morning, rain or shine.

He also saw that the rules were strictly adhered to. For example, all paths should be three feet wide. It is an historical English trait, I have observed over the years, that land will be grabbed anywhere, even if it means scraping as little as two or three inches off a path between allotments to enlarge your own plot. In the past this has led to rows of vendetta proportions between the plot holders either side of an ever narrowing path. The hardest role of holding allotment office is the moment of adjudication. Recently we have had at least four disputes involving greenhouses. Usually the person who put up the greenhouse is giving up their plot, either through moving house, or age or ill health, and they want financial payment from the new plot holder for their greenhouse, but we argue as an Association that they have the choice to take the greenhouse away with them. Sometimes they agree to do this, but then cause inconvenience to the new incumbent by delaying the removal. They ask us for a month or so to remove the structure, but, of course, never do. All this time we have to instruct the newcomer not to use the greenhouse—a ridiculous situation.

There was an even worse escalation of a greenhouse dispute where the person involved was leaving the plot after many years and disputes. When the new plot holder arrived they found that all the glass in the greenhouse had been smashed. The previous owner denied this piece of vandalism. To this day we have an empty greenhouse on another plot, whose owner was offered £50 by the Association just to settle the dispute, but in the end our cheque was returned. This particular row has recently been solved by her death

This is the negative side of the job, when you hear all the complaints and receive little praise for what you think the committee is achieving. What is encouraging is how well all our seventeen different nationalities usually get on together, and how we learn from each other's styles of gardening, and what is going on in the area through gossip and rumour. We were first to discover Mayor Livingstone's plans to enlarge the Congestion charge area, because some of our Irish members knew the men who were secretly doing the measuring. We also knew that 'consultation' with the public would be a charade and it would happen anyway, which the Mayor himself later admitted. We also hear from General Safi, ex-protector of the King of Afghanistan, far more about what is happening, or should be, in Afghanistan than from whoever is Foreign Secretary of the moment.

As the days shorten and may stay warm, so the nights lengthen and grow colder. This finishes off what might be left of the tomatoes that haven't got the blight already. This started, ironically, on the organic plot of David Bays and Maureen, and gradually spread across the plots. It is all to do with the extremes of temperature, which is why right now there is hardly a tomato left that has not turned brown at the top or its base. The only thing to do now is to pick the green ones that are left before they are attacked and use them to make chutney.

This is the second busiest time of the year for our shop as we put on sale winter sets of red and white onions and aqua dulce broad bean seeds that can be sown at the end of October. For the next four Sundays, after the AGM in October, the rents have to be paid by each plot holder, who must come to the shop to do this.

In the shop not so many people buy the broad beans as the onion sets, yet it is thought that autumn-planted broad beans do not attract the dreaded black fly that can quickly ruin your crop. Normally there are two good ways of keeping the black fly at bay. The first is to pinch out their tops when the beans are fully grown. This is usually the area first infested by black fly, who then spread down the stem of each plant as they inhabit and feast off it. Country vegetable gardeners tend to eat the pinched-out tops, regarding them as a delicacy. Mind you, I presume they wouldn't have been infested with black fly. The other way I have mentioned before, and that is to give them a dowsing of water mixed with washing-up liquid. I always plant several rows of broad beans in the autumn, so as to have them early the next season. There is nothing like the taste of the first broad beans, a world away from those bullet-like specimens you used to get in school dinners, or find on sale these days at supermarkets.

It is pretty cold sitting in the shipping container in the autumn, and John and Doreen have been given an old gas bottle heater, plus John's ingenious battery lamp which is strung above them. But they still need good, thick coats, and maybe even a rug over Doreen's knees as she enters each paying plot holder in her book, and checks if they have got their yellow membership card with all our rules on the back.

At one time, when the dreaded Park Club were planning one of their expansions, they said that in return for allowing an electric cable to be brought through our land, we could run a lead into our container, as it has all the wherewithal inside to be connected to the mains and provide its own lighting and heating system. But that plan did not go ahead, so John and Doreen still have to rely on the basics.

Autumn is altogether a busy time, because there is the digging to be done. Charlie Rycroft is first to dig half his plot and put his onions in as soon as they arrive in the shop. Joe notes that he has slowed up a bit these days, and he no longer has that bustling walk that we are all used to, but I say to Joe, 'A man of that age has a right to slow up a bit.' However, when we cut the long hedge for the last time this year, Charlie will still be up perched on top of his ladder clipping away the top of the hedge that could not be reached from outside!

One lunchtime I had to go up to my plot, because I had a six-pinter of golden liquid to pour on the last of the season's grass I have just distributed around my five compost bins. There is also a very large bag of kitchen waste. It is just past lunchtime, and I see Les coming out of Joe's shed and throwing the dregs of a mug of tea across the path. With him, as usual, is his bright little terrier dog, but as I pass Stewart's shed another small, black dog comes running up towards me. It is very friendly, and immediately lets me tickle its head. As it goes running off to join Les and his little terrier I presume that he has got himself a second dog. He explains that he found this dog wandering up and down a busy road just around the corner, so he brought it into the allotments. Now Joe was putting together a rope lead and collar, because it did not appear to have a collar of its own.

Les said that when he was taking his own dog for a walk yesterday in Acton Park, there was a notice offering a £500 reward for the return of a pedigree dog. I was told by one of the clerks at west London court that there had been a lot of 'dog napping' in west London of late. Money was demanded for the return of the dog. Meanwhile, Les was wondering what to do with this very pleasant little dog. 'It would suit you,' I said to Joe. I will not print his reply. Suffice to say he didn't want this, or any other dog! He is more worried about the whereabouts of his wheelbarrow. It is almost a communal one as anyone can use it for transporting manure and chippings to and from their plot.

*　　　*　　　*

Les reports that he had heard the dog was missing from the nearby council flats in Trinity Way. He found a woman who purported to be the owner and handed over the dog. But there was a slight complication

162

because someone else also said it might have been their dog. By then Les had done enough good deeds, and presumably the dog was safe and being fed.

Nearly every day someone rings up wanting an allotment, but today I got an unusual call from a woman in Cambridge, who had found me through Stephen Cole, Ealing's Allotment officer. She had a relative who was seriously ill, and wanted to contact someone who had at one time been one of her closest friends and shared an allotment with her. Her name was simply Jane, and she would now be in her mid-fifties or sixties. I am afraid the only Jane I know is young Jayne, one of the BBC girls. She did not fit the bill. As no one has heard of her I will have to make more enquiries.

It is certainly a busy time for octogenarians. Joe tells me that Jonjo will be eighty this week. I ask where the party will be, and Joe says he has already asked Jonjo about this and he got a spluttered reply about him spending the time at home, and two friends visiting him. No doubt he will have time to share a drink or two with Stewart outside his shed. Joe measures the time they have been drinking by the volume of their conversation. 'The volume's up tonight,' he will says rather roguishly. Jonjo is proud of how much work he still does. Every morning he sweeps out a betting shop and he also cycles miles a week collecting money for a pools firm.

163

I have to attend my first meeting as a member of the London Food Link. When I arrive at City Hall, the home of the Greater London Authority just below Tower Bridge, the identification card I had to pin on my lapel read 'Michael Wale. London Food Link. Allotment Activist'. It was the second line that drew people to talk to me. There was a very interesting cross-section of people there. We were asked not to sit in lines, but for eight or more to sit down at one of the many tables spread across the room. I was soon sitting down with members of the National Farmers' Union, the National Health Service, and a consumers' representative as well as representatives from Staffordshire County Council and Glasgow. I was approached also by a member of Groundwork, a non-government organisation, who said she would get in touch with their west London representative to help us in our bid to get allotments in the nearby park, behind the Perryn flats which are opposite our main site.

It was encouraging to note the interest the National Health Service has in allotments, finding that they are extremely therapeutic for patients who may have mental health problems. They liked my slogan Join A Real Health Club. Get An Allotment, and someone asked if they could use it. The more good publicity allotments get the better, and the more they become part of the mainstream at meetings like this the better.

The AGM beckons, and I ring John Kirby, our previous chairman who is still a member of the Acton Vale Social Club, to see if he can find us a date when they can let us hold our meeting there, as we have for some years. John warns that they are holding some Trafalgar celebrations the week I have requested. I wasn't aware that Shepherd's Bush has links with Nelson and his navy!

John Kirby, who has not been in the best of health, resigned from the chairmanship last year. John, an ex-prison officer and union leader at Wormwood Scrubs would like to say a few words at our meeting, and I agree. He did a lot of work for the Association when he was chairman during our dispute with the Park Club, and we used to hold Extraordinary General Meetings downstairs at the same club.

Last year's meeting started with a crisis. John is responsible for printing the agenda and he was not well, and at the last moment was unable to attend. The agenda is handed out to members as they arrive, together with the annual financial statement, and the new catalogue from Tuckers. We are usually the first people in the country to receive their new catalogue. Fortunately John's wife had printed out the agendas, and I popped round to collect them. To be honest I really do fear AGM night. It is a big worry until it is all over.

Rachel Pepper chaired for the evening as Bill Geddes had gone to Scotland. Rachel is a very able organiser, and helps run the Vale estate's Residents' Association. She lives on the estate, and takes a very active part, is a wonderful organiser, took an allotment on the Vale site, and advises us how to apply for and get grants to improve our sites. She was behind getting financial funding for part of the total cost of installing the new water system, as well as getting new sheds. For good measure she has just taken her Masters degree. She chairs the meeting superbly, and as a matter of fact a lot of people who have never spoken before do just that.

Meanwhile, this year Bill Geddes has become aware that there are questions as to why the agreement between Ealing Council and the Park Club has not been signed. Under a Section 106 agreement this guarantees us ninety years' protection, rent free with various other promises. This agreement was announced at an open meeting of the Planning Committee in Ealing Town Hall nearly three years ago. All sorts of excuses have been found by each side not to sign. One of our members says that he would like to take it up directly with the Park Club. I am worried that a verbal hand grenade could cause us more problems. The threat of the three-month notice from the Park Club nearly brought about our total extinction and the softly softly policy saved us. However, I have emailed our local Labour councillor Paul Woodgate pressing him to get me some information. I have warned him in a previous email that we may soon have to go public about all this. Conveniently for us London has its local council elections next spring, when no doubt all sorts of promises will be made locally to the allotment movement.

Bill Geddes, having worked in local government, is making enquiries at council level to find when, and if, the council are going to bring this long drawn-out process to a satisfactory conclusion for us.

The more immediate problem ahead is the installation of a huge new water system on the Perryn and Chestnuts combined sites. Joe is in charge, and has worked out a strategy. We needed to completely renew all the pipes which were metal, leaking, and dating back many, many, years. We also wanted water to be quickly available to each site through nearby water tanks with taps. At the moment there is no pattern at all, and you might have to walk a quite a distance to the nearest water tank. So Joe decided there should be one tank situated between four plots, with a tap.

Even before work had started we received a financial shock, when Thames Water demanded £1,500 for bringing the water supply across Bromyard Avenue, the road outside. The reason for shifting the point of entry was that ever since we could remember, the water supply came in on the far side of the site, through a hedge and land belonging to a church hall. Not only did it have no pressure but one hot summer in the past our supply was inadvertently turned off, and for two or three weeks we could not work out why we had no water!

There are bound to be complaints aplenty now as the digger encroaches by at least a couple of feet onto the plots next to the paths that are being dug up for the new water pipes. They have to be two feet six inches deep to comply with the rules of Thames Water. As for my own plot the digger did take away quite a bit of land. Worse still, the clay from beneath was put back on top, so that I was left with a hard crust about nine inches thick. For once the old, but untrue, adage about planting potatoes so that they did the work in the soil would be true. It is the plot holder who does all the work in reality: the autumn digging, the spring redigging, the digging of trenches to put the potatoes in, then earthing them up. All the potatoes have to do is grow! And it is the plot holder who has to dig them up and return the earth to a flat surface. This is necessary in order to return the ghastly orange-coloured clay to where it belongs.

The original water system was all metal pipes and was prone to rust and leak. Nowadays there are blue plastic pipes, which come in a roll and unfurl neatly into the trench. Joe, John and Michael, from the Bromyard site, make it look easy. I keep well away, apart from making visits to admire their work.

As I have said, in the new scheme of things it was planned to provide one water tank with a tap for each four plots. We needed 425 metres of pipe. Then we had to pay £1,200 for taps, and another £400 for stopcocks. The mini-digger came with a driver, and he needed thirty-two hours to dig all the trenches, and then another eight to fill them in again once the pipes had been laid and inspected. Although it was autumn now, we all feared that someone would come up to the site and fall into an open trench. The trenches had to remain open until the first inspection by Thames Water, to check that they were deep enough.

When I had first negotiated all this with the water board, I explained that we were not a building site, which is what they were used to dealing with. They were not used to allotment sites, a phenomenon that did not find a place in their paperwork. So despite explaining to them that the trenches should be inspected and filled in as soon as possible, because of the danger to our plot holders, they still seemed to class us as a building site, and said that we would have to await inspection until all the trenches had been dug. Until then, they must all be left open.

Meanwhile, the team doing the work from our end—Joe, John, Michael, plus Les and his little terrier—laid the pipe, made sure no clay got into it, carefully pushed each fitting into place, and every few feet measured the trench depth with their measuring stick. As for our friendly man with the digger, he was kept well filled with sandwiches and tea, put together in Joe's shed.

And so came the day of the first inspection. Thankfully it was raining. Not that we had anything to hide, but we did not want an inspector nosing around our plot for too long finding fault where there was none, as officials are apt to do. Allotment sites are rightly secretive places. The inspector was not going to be out of his van long on such a morning with the rain pouring down. He made a fairly brief inspection and said that everything was all right. He also hinted that the final inspection would not find much wrong either. We retired to Joe's shed with the first obstacle cleared.

I'm afraid our celebrations were short-lived, because when the same man returned for the final inspection, on a dry, slightly warmer day, he said that it was not good enough just to have stopcocks but we must have non-returnable taps as well. As the taps had all been joined up to standpipes, which had been joined to the pipes below, a lot of work had to be undone. We also had to spend several hundreds of pounds more for the alterations to the taps. The reason is so that no water from the allotments can go back into the mains. Joe said this had already been done and asked the inspector to explain his reasons. But he was merely told that this was what it said in the book. And so it was.

The standpipes had been the hardest part of Joe, Michael and John's work. They had to make them stand upright and firm. Each of the seventeen different stand-pipes and taps had to be taken to bits and refitted with their box-like wooden surrounds that Joe had made so carefully. We all despaired, and at one moment actually felt defeated. We wondered if we could continue. More money to be spent, yet more work for our hard unpaid workforce. Depression all around.

Joe went back to the drawing board in his mind, and worked out a way to solve the problem. Thames Water arrived to dig up the road. In fact they only had to dig halfway across, but we had already paid the £1,500 weeks before. They worked for a maximum of just over two hours, before connecting our new system up to the mains.

Eventually, some days later, the inspector returned and approved the whole piece of work. Once again it was raining heavily and he seemed reluctant to leave the warmth of his van. He did not spend long to give us the final clearance. This time there was relief all around. All there was left to do now, ironically, was to turn the water off, so that if and when the frosts came the system would not suffer any fatal freeze-ups. Also it puts a stop to the ever-rising water bills.

I had planned to explain our water installation to an Allotment Regeneration get-together at King's College. Having attended a morning workshop I decided I did not want to stay any longer. There were too many diverse views from too many diverse backgrounds. I think I have had enough workshops. They are the flavour of our time, rather like New Labour's fixation with 'initiatives', and unless well addressed and forcefully led with direction I can do without them. So just before lunch I left.

There is a certain pecking order when it comes to being invited into someone's shed for tea regularly, occasionally, or not at all. In the years before what has become known as our 'Troubles', a fried breakfast used to be served in Dave Wheeler's hut: sausage, egg and bacon. Delicious. But in those days I was not a member of the senior circle. Gradually, I was invited to have tea with John Bowtacz, a Ukrainian who came to Britain, via Germany, just after the Second World War. You would not have guessed he had lived and worked in London so long with his thick, guttural accent, at times difficult to understand. He worked in local factories like CAV and Wall's. He appeared like something out of a Second World War movie, with a big rubber apron tied around him and a fur hat with large flaps dropped down over his ears in cold or wet weather. He was gracious, and very respectful towards women, who rather frightened him. He was also a well-read and intelligent man, who felt the Britain that he had come to after the war had deteriorated in manners, cleanliness and respect for the elderly. He also hated pop music, being a lover of the classics, and was blessed until quite late in his life with a beautiful tenor voice. He loved opera. He also loved the country of his birth, the Ukraine. He would teach me to pronounce Kiev properly, ask about the Ukrainian soccer star Shevchenko, and every now and again attend a Ukrainian event of visiting choirs or orchestras.

He would speak little about his past, but I gleaned that he was taken from his native country to Austria as the Hitler regime took over. In those early days he worked on a farm, and judging by his horticultural skills, he was highly skilful. He admitted the woman farmer in charge would like to have kept him there, but for some reason he was moved on to work in Munich, right up to the end of the war and the bombing by the RAF. It seemed at the end he not only lived on very little but in very uncomfortable circumstances.

In his early life in Britain he was very involved in the Roman Catholic Church, becoming a server to bishops and other Church dignitaries. He sang in choirs, and he was part of the Church. But in his later years he became very embittered about religion and had become an atheist. It was no exaggeration to say he now hated the Catholic Church. I do not know why. He also talked of the huge influence in Britain of the Freemasons. It became an obsession with him. He claimed to have unearthed a secret Freemason book that had revealed to him all their secrets. He was so fearful of what he had discovered that he would not impart the information to me except to say, 'Beware, they are everywhere.' They are not on the allotments as far as I know. But in the old days you may well have got an allotment by giving the right man the right handshake.

More importantly John shaped the allotments around him. First he constructed a shed beneath an elderly pear tree, and he was so trusted by bird life that the most secretive and shy of all birds, the wren, built a nest above the door of his shed. We would have to sit inside very quietly when these tiny birds came and went, first with nesting materials and then with tiny insects to feed their young.

*   *   *

174

It was an honour to be accepted to have tea with John. You knew you had arrived when he put your initials on the bottom of a mug. He was very punctilious about who drank out of which mug or cup. Woe betide if you drank out of the wrong mug. You would not be drinking in his shed again. In fact it wasn't a shed, more of a plastic covered greenhouse, so he could nurture his cuttings during the winter period, and encourage them to a future with the aid of a paraffin heater.

It was John who had fixed up our first source of manure, always the biggest problem for an inner-city plot holder. It came from an unlikely background. The owner of a fish and chip shop around the corner kept racing pigeons in a loft on his roof. This was only a hundred yards or so from the busy A40. The fish and chips were of a high order, fried in the old-fashioned way on a coal-heated fryer, and the fish brought all the way from Scotland. The interior of the shop was wonderfully old-fashioned, all green and white tiles, and here and there a large picture of one of the owner's successful racing pigeons.

Pigeon manure is very acidic, and is best kept for a year in a black bag. Even then not many plants like it, except for broad beans which would positively wallow in it, even when it was fresh. Strangely, runner beans have never liked it at any stage.

One of our Italian group at the time, Mario,

said that John's was not the real pigeon manure. He had found a man around the corner who trained champions, and therefore their manure was far superior. Mario and John had a special relationship. John used Mario almost as his servant, and instructed him how to put his roof back on his shed or greenhouse. Or to construct containers for plants. They would frequently disagree as to how a job should be done. Mario was a great one for tying things together with wire or string, whereas John had the mind of an engineer and would wish things to be secured into position permanently, and would work out a way of dovetailing their wooden surfaces together. 'Poor Mario,' he would say with pious mock pity, out of the other man's hearing.

The search for manure took many twists and turns. I knew a racing trainer in Epsom, Philip Mitchell, whose stables were near the start of the Derby, on the far side of the Downs. One day a friend said he had access to a trailer, so off we went to Epsom. We loaded it up from the stable's muck heap and took our prized load back to East Acton. Later when I rang to thank him Philip said that he had noted the date of the proposed collection was April 1st, and thought the whole thing was an elaborate April Fool's joke.

Two Irish members thought they could go one better when the circus came to nearby

Acton Park. It was the last year that animals were permitted to perform with circuses in London, and the sought-after prize was the elephant dung. They claimed that because it was so large, and produced by vegetarians, it would help them to grow even bigger crops.

They barrowed several loads around, and certainly their muck heap was the largest that had been seen for some time. As for the end product, their leeks were the same size as ever.

This year I decided we needed a regular source, as we were beginning to run things far more professionally. We had a relationship with a nun who ran a riding school for the disabled on Wormwood Scrubs, but the wheels literally fell off their transport. No one could find the right wheels to replace their elderly trailer so the supply stopped. Alf Barnes suggested I ring the barracks at Knightsbridge as he had heard they would deliver direct, the results of the excretions of the Household Cavalry horses. I rang up Knightsbridge barracks and was put through to someone who was obviously an officer. When I explained what I was after it was as if I'd said that I wished to make love to his wife. Curtly he suggested this was a case for the subalterns, and I was handed abruptly down the chain of command to someone who could not command at all. At least he was polite and informative, saying that the Knightsbridge barracks had a contract to deliver all their manure to Kew Gardens.

He suggested that I ring Buckingham Palace, which is precisely what I did. They were very pleasant and put me through to the Royal gardener, Mark Lowe. I almost asked to be put through to the Royal potting shed, but I thought this might end any relationship I was hoping to set up. Mark Lowe was charming and said that London allotments did have the right to apply for deliveries of Royal manure free of charge. He put us on the list, and that was the start of what is still our regular supplier. All I have to do is to ring up the driver on his mobile and say we need some more. There are hold-ups at some points in the year, as the horses actually go on holiday! International politics can also intervene, as when President George Bush came to stay at Buckingham Palace. The security was so tight that even the manure lorry was confined to barracks for a few days.

It always impresses new plot holders that they are actually using Royal manure. It is, of course, of very good order, or should I say odour? Sometimes it is wonderfully full of straw; other times there is quite a bit of hay in it; otherwise it is shavings. Obviously the bedding of these equine aristocrats is changed at least twice a day, if not more.

The presence of the thriving Italian colony on our site was down to Mario who has had a plot for over thirty years, and yet still spoke in broken English as if he had just arrived from Italy. When he retired a few years ago, he spent all his time from breakfast until supper time on the allotments. Always accompanied by his dog Rudi, and quite often visited by his wife, who shared a carefully prepared lunch with him of Italian meats and bread, plus some of the fresh basil that he grew in his shed-cum-greenhouse. He grew several varieties of basil in old fish boxes filled with compost.

Two years ago he suffered stomach pains, but was put right after an operation at the nearby Hammersmith Hospital. Mario made a remarkable recovery, and returned to his daily programme of non-stop physical work as well as offering a torrent of well-meant advice for the rest of us in his incomprehensible English. Having suffered moan after moan from plot holders, about the most minor matters, and driven mad by grumbles in general at the time, I proposed that Mario should become plot representative for our section. He was as delighted as I. And the grumblers? Well, they gave up after a few minutes of trying to understand what Mario was talking about!

Mario was renowned for not going on holiday but, over the past two years, after his initial illness, went back to Italy and other places, and we noted that Rudi, who remained behind, was very much a one-man dog. He seemed very sad for the whole time his owner was absent, although he was taken for walks. He looked thin, and obviously went off his food at these times.

One day, soon after his return, Mario followed me along the line I was digging, rather like an inquisitive robin waiting for the first worm to surface. He confided in me that the pain of two years ago had returned, and he pointed to an area of his stomach. He did not know the cause, as all the hospital tests had been all right.

A few weeks later he had visibly lost a lot of weight and admitted to feeling weak, saying that he only really had enough energy to walk Rudi up to the allotment and back. Once here he would sit down, but not do any work. His wife would always appear with him. She has always kept a loving eye on him, especially after his first illness when the doctors ordered him not to do too much physical work. For Mario this proved to be almost impossible, and so he would work away physically at a task until he would be warned that his wife was arriving at the gate, and he would stop and return to his greenhouse of a hut, and sit down as if he had been resting all the time

When Mario said that he had to go back into hospital I feared the worst. And the worst it, indeed, turned out to be. It was reflected in a short note fixed some days later to the notice board by the gate. It told of his death, and gave the date of the funeral.

There was a huge turnout for his funeral and, movingly, the hearse drove up to the allotments and paused before it continued on its way.

There was another death that was to affect particularly those of us on the committee. I had rung the Hogarth Club one Monday and asked for Patrick, because the fencing that the Park Club had agreed to give us in return for our membership installing it, had not arrived. The receptionist passed me on to someone I had only spoken to once or twice before. 'Haven't you heard?' he asked, 'Patrick was killed at the weekend.' He had been on holiday in the Seychelles with his wife and three children. It was the last evening, and he had gone swimming, but a freak current had carried him beneath a rock and he had drowned. Patrick had been such an ally to us, and smoothed the path from head-on enmity to an understanding relationship. He was a remarkable person and practising Christian. I sent two members, Joe Hughes and John Roberts, to his funeral in Chiswick, because I had a business appointment. They reported that the church had been crammed, the service quite long but beautiful, with the appearance of the choir from Patrick's Cambridge college. I felt that his father would be greatly affected, as indeed I heard he was. I wrote him a personal letter of condolence.

Leading up to the AGM Bill Geddes and Joe Hughes had been very busy touring all the plots, and Bill had made several notes, blacklisting several people for not caring for their plots. We are back to the old poser as to why some people bother to take a plot, when they might dig it, plant something, and then never visit it again, not even to harvest what they planted. Bill is much stricter than the committee has dared to be in the past, and awards marks for each plot. I fear I might not get top marks. I am not sure I like all this marking business; it smacks of all those New Labour leagues and ticked boxes. I think it is much more important to remove people who do not actually use their allotment. An allotment association is a group of friends, who should meet on their sites regularly, not stay away. One trick of a non-attendee is to pay their rent by cheque, even before it is due. Unfortunately John Roberts has fallen for just such a ploy. We are now drawing up a blacklist and will refuse to take payment from certain people, thus ending their membership and tenancy of their plot

This plan comes into force from the first Sunday following the AGM when over the next four Sundays payments have to be made. We expect our stricter policy will cause trouble, and Joe and others have promised to keep alongside Doreen as she ticks off membership cards and takes the money.

One plot in particular has caused us a lot of trouble, because it is right by the main gates, and is always seen by passers-by, who want an allotment. When they are told there is a lengthy waiting list they do not believe us, and point, quite rightly, at this huge unused site right there by the gate. Worse was that the person to whom the plot belonged had been one of our best gardeners for many years but he moved out of London. When the committee sent out a warning letter relatives would arrive, quickly fulfil our rules by digging the whole plot over, then leave and never come back. So it just returned to the weed-covered plot it had been before we sent out our warning.

Until now our hands have been tied, because we were told the plot holder had been in hospital, and that he'd had to move out of London, but would be returning. On the first payment Sunday he turned up and we had a long, relaxed and friendly talk. It does appear that he has been spending a lot of time out of London. He has also had leg trouble, which will certainly not improve his prospects for digging. Indeed, he admits that he will not be able to dig at all, but that a relative would come in and help him. We point out that this is not in the spirit of having an allotment. He says he will let us know in a week's time whether he wants to take it on again. Joe reckons that at last the plot will be handed back to us.

A week later it is given up at last, and we decide to divide it, as part of our new policy of letting several half-plots to newcomers, and people who might not want to commit themselves to what can be a quite daunting task when faced with digging a full-sized plot.

Having an allotment means a lot more work than the person brought up watching gardening on television realises. The trouble with television gardening is that it all seems so easy, with no physical effort required. In reality, to keep a plot producing for your family you need at least an hour a day on it. It is quite amazing what you can do during an hour a day, but the digging is the drawback.

The good thing about the month-long Sunday payment period is that it boosts the onion sales in the shop, and this year's reintroduction by Tuckers of winter red onions has proved to be just what our members wanted. We only ordered half a sack, but now we have had to go back and order all that Tuckers have left. Tuckers gave up red onion sets because they had so many complaints about them going quickly to seed. But then they found a supplier who solved the problem. I bought some as it is true that all gardeners like to try something new.

In the past our own allotment association did not embrace change, preferring the ordinary fare of the usual potatoes, runner beans and white onions. All that has changed. We get asked for Pink Fir Apple potatoes, whose shapes bring back memories of Esther Rantzen's television show where the strange genitalian shape of some vegetables always drew a big laugh from the audience. Plant a Pink Fir Apple and you will have a talking point for as long as it remains on the plate!

Debra is always trying out new things, grown patiently from seed. I think she has started the next vegetable craze with her success with climbing French dwarf beans. The growing conditions in the last three years have not produced the best of runner beans, because they seem to come quickly and dry out quickly. In fact they need a lot of water, and London's hard fluoride tap water does not really seem to satisfy plants. Watering from the hose or the can, unless it is rainwater from one of my ex-oil tanks, is no substitute for a really good downpour. There just seems to be less and less rain in high summer, due no doubt to the dreaded global warming. But at the end of the summer everyone admired Debra's climbing dwarf French beans, because they have the advantage over French beans in that they do not trail on the ground, attracting slugs and snails, or get muddy should there be a rare fall of rain.

We harnessed some of Debra's energy to help us with a problem plot. In the beginning it was really good but the plot holder gave it up. There followed a man who smoked incessantly and, not surprisingly, was suffering medically as a result, and he could not actually do much physical work. On some days he could hardly breathe. He did install a permanent park-type seat for him and his wife to sit on when they came. However, the seat caused one of those rows that blow up on an allotment occasionally. His wife arrived one day to find someone else sitting on their seat. Not the greatest crime, but she took great exception to it. Not long after this incident he died. And his wife did not come anymore. Now and again one of us would sit on the controversial seat recalling the incident and sadly remembering the pleasant man who had died through smoking too much.

Next came a local flat dweller, a pleasant West Indian. Yet gradually his visits became less and less frequent, with the plot deteriorating. At best he only dug half of it, and replied to any criticism that it was his land and he could do what he liked with it. None of us agreed with this, but did not wish to start another argument on a plot that seemed cursed.

In the end he said he would give it up, but wanted his money back for the greenhouse, for which he said he had given the previous owner £100. He also wanted to sell his tools. This was the classic greenhouse situation. The committee's feeling was that either he dismantled the greenhouse and took it away, or it was left to the next incumbents for nothing. I wish there had been an Allotment Act that spelt out that the welfare of the plot was above that of any human individual!

By this stage I had had one of my great ideas, which was to go spectacularly wrong. A charity had written to us saying that they dealt with homeless people, and they thought an allotment would help as part of their rehabilitation. They guaranteed that at any time these people were on the plot they would be accompanied by supervisors. The supervisors were mainly young girls who were very pleasant but, naturally, did not understand much about allotment gardening. Joe and John dealt with that, however, with their usual good humour and advice, and the whole scheme got underway. I had always felt we should do something for those less fortunate than ourselves. I had also noted that in Birmingham, allotments were used as part of the therapy for people with mental health problems, and were also taken by the Social Services department to help people get something out of what might have been an empty life.

We told the West Indian that his greenhouse and plot was going to be used for a charity, and that he would surely like to be part of this move. The Association, therefore, would give him £40 for the greenhouse, and the rather old tools within it. He agreed.

Quite soon there were three or four men at work, under the watchful eyes of their supervisor, for the day. But things did not seem to go very well as far as the gardening was concerned. There was one quite keen young man, but the others did not seem to share his enthusiasm, and soon stories were reaching the committee of drunkenness, members of the public being insulted through the fence, and bad language being used within the hearing of Mario's wife. Fortunately the charity decided to leave before we had to make a decision ourselves. The whole experience was a great pity, and made my 'great idea' look rather foolish, and has set the committee back should we wish to link up with a charity in the future.

So the long-term result was an awful plot with a history of neglect. That is why we sent for Debra. She patched up the half-broken greenhouse and used it to grow her trays of seeds, of which there were many. Gradually she dug the plot back into shape, but even she found it a challenge.

The four-week payment ended, the money was all collected, and the defaulters had been weeded out by Doreen and John, sitting each Sunday getting colder and colder as winter approached rather too quickly. The onions were all sold, which is a relief. There is now one big job left and that is to formulate the potato order for the next spring. The order has to be put in soon to guarantee that we get exactly what we want. But that is a job for the winter.

For now John and Joe heave the heavy double doors of the shipping container shop closed for the last time this season, and lock it up until the following February.

Autumn Recipe

Courgettes. I like them done two ways. Either sliced an inch thick and baked in the oven with a drizzle of olive oil and crushed garlic on top of each slice, or fried gently in a pan and served with grated cheese sprinkled over the top.

Autumn/Winter

We are planning to 'twin' our allotments with those in Calais, partly to reinforce our strength as an organisation, and discourage any other would-be property predators.

In reality it is so that we can travel to France and have a jolly good meal and drink with kindred spirits, and buy seeds. Jerome, who is in charge of this mission, has received three letters of approval from the five different allotment associations in Calais.

Jerome was born in France, and is a fluent French speaker. His father married a Geordie and the family moved to Newcastle-upon-Tyne, before Jerome came south to London, where he is a lecturer. In his spare time, besides being an excellent allotment gardener with his teacher partner Carol, he runs the London branch of the Newcastle United supporters' club. He quite often travels up on a Saturday to see Newcastle play at St James's Park.

The whole 'twinning' process, which was another of my wretched 'good' ideas, has taken ages, because the French take weeks and weeks to reply to our letters. No doubt it will happen eventually, although the one we have chosen, because it seems to be the most central, wants to know what the process will involve: now Jerome and I have got to invent something. A mission statement of allotment gardening, perhaps, we suggest to each other on his plot, falling about with laughter at the thought.

The news from those who have observed the allotments in Calais brings ominous reports about high standards of uniformity, and very neat huts, for each immaculately tended plot. The whole thing about British allotments is the shed culture. In other words, every shed is different, made from different materials, having a character expressing that of its owner. My own was built by my faithful co-committee members, far more talented at practical allotment matters than I am, John Roberts, and Joe Hughes.

We have four sites that make up the total area of allotments run by the Acton Gardening Association. One of them is now surrounded by the Virgin Health Club, and during its construction John Roberts, who runs that site, found out that most of the extremely good wood and other waste was due to be taken away and burned.

One structure housed the electrics. When Virgin had finished their building work it had served its purpose, was taken to bits and moved onto my site. John and Joe got to work. The result is that I have a purpose-built shed, with a writing desk before me, with windows overlooking not only my plot, but, in the far distance, I can see anyone who comes through the gate.

Even better, I can sit unobserved, and realise why I do not need a second home in the country. I could be miles away from the inner city right here as I look out on a fox grooming itself beneath the ancient yew tree, and listen to the birdsong and look for my favourite robin, which probably will not reveal himself until I go out and do some digging.

Digging. Sometimes I like it, sometimes I loathe it. The most satisfying thing about it is that at the end of a session you can actually see what you have done, and how much you have progressed. On the other hand you can still see how much there is left to do. That is winter digging for you. Well, it's something to do. A reason to go to the allotment at weekends as the days shorten depressingly. A time to swap trainers for heavier leather boots, with feet now warmed by wearing Norwegian sailors' socks. Heavier trousers and a mud-spattered coat complete the down at heel look!

The winter started off wet, raining nearly every day, which delays the digging, making it very frustrating. At least it leaves time to study the seed catalogues—not that anyone beats Tuckers for price and variety of seeds. John will be ready soon with his shopping list, and I have found a cheap source of fruit trees, after doing an interview for an Internet site. I write the weekly leading article for 50Connect, a portal for the over-fifties. The reason was Apple Day. I wanted to find a fruit farmer who earned a living by growing different sorts of British apples than were offered for sale in the supermarkets.

The Small family based at Charlton Orchards in Creech St Michael, near Taunton in Somerset, fulfilled the spec. They are unusual in that they were not originally a farming family. Robin Small spent a long time in the navy, and when he left he and his wife June decided to have a lifestyle change, sell up their home in Buckinghamshire between Marlow and High Wycombe and move to Somerset to grow apples.

Until four years ago the family had to rely upon the supermarkets for their livelihood. But with the rise of the farmers' markets movement they decided to change course, and sell the apples from their forty-five acres locally, and also by post. They have set up two farmers' markets in Taunton and Bridgwater, which they run as producers' cooperatives.

The Smalls grow no less than thirty-five varieties of English apples, some of them like the nutty-tasting Ashmeads Kernel, dating back three hundred years. That was not in the list they sent me, but there was the Orlean Reinette. By the time I'd done the rounds I had an order for over twenty trees, including pears and plums, as well as figs for

194

Debra and me.

They duly arrived and the Smalls' advice was not to put them in a bucket of water, as most people have told me in the past but dig a hole in the ground and put them all in root first, and they will be happy until you want to plant them out in their permanent positions.

Another, much more expensive tree has been commissioned for us to buy and plant on the Vale estate, which faces onto the Vale site. Groundwork are paying £170 for a copper beech, which is already ten foot tall, and arrived in its own root ball. We provided a bag of organic compost to put around it when it was planted to celebrate the official opening of the new community centre, which is linked with the new all-weather sports facility that we have helped the Vale's residents' committee in their fight to achieve. Rachel Pepper has driven the two projects aided by Jim Wong.

John Roberts or I have tried to attend every meeting as part of my belief that the allotment movement in the past had been too inward-looking, too focused on its own affairs. But now the time has come to involve ourselves with other groups out there in the local community. That is why we had become involved with our nearest neighbours, the Vale estate, who had also been affected by the building of the Park Club, losing land used for walking their dogs, playing football and training by QPR coaches in the holidays. The rest of the land, open to local people, vanished when the local council sold out to the Virgin Health Club. Now they have nothing. So we backed a plan to make an all-weather, floodlit area for sport. Virgin had to give a certain sum of money to Ealing Council for the right to take over the council's fading leisure centre, and totally rebuild it and the surrounding area.

A battle developed over the amount of money the council would give to the Vale for the new sports facilities and a new community centre. After many months, the Vale's residents won, and the tree to commemorate it would be planted in the children's play area.

I do recall that during one of the meetings when the subject of the tree was on the agenda, someone asked if we could find a tree that birds would not sit in and mess on people below. John Roberts and I had to explain that birds, like trees, were all part of nature that we should always welcome right here in inner-city west London.

We got several children to plant the tree, thinking that they would be responsible for it and, therefore, protect it. Organising and planting the tree, during this winter period, relieved part of the gloom as the days began to close in.

Another welcome way of putting off the real gloom of winter was a visit to Peter Springall, who has two plots on an enormous allotment site owned by Bexley Council on a slope leading down the hill from the original Crystal Palace. Peter is an expert on bee-keeping, and also, even more importantly these days, on growing vines, and making his own wine. He makes nearly four hundred bottles a year. Two years ago he gave me a cutting from one of his vines, which has grown and now has produced its first grapes. Not enough for me to make wine myself, but at least I can take the grapes over to Peter and he can include them in his 2004 vintage: Chateau Sydenham, as I have named it.

It was one of those sunny, cold, but dry winter days that gives rise to the saying 'Indian summer'; clear, crisp energising. Peter is in his eighties, and he has to repeat this because I don't believe him! He is far too energetic and active for that age, but here he is today crushing his grapes in a machine that he made himself from various cannibalised pieces of other machinery. He spent a lifetime working as an engineer, and for much of that time his hobby was bee-keeping. In fact his answerphone still says: 'This is Peter the bee-keeper.' He still has some hives on one plot just in front of the pride of his allotment life, a forty-foot-long vine that he brought originally from a Kent nursery. Now he has trained it across the path and back. He used to travel to Europe with the bee-keeping club, and that is how he became interested in drinking wine, and finding out how it was produced. He used to slip away from the bee-keepers and ask questions in vineyards about vine-culture. When he started growing vines on his allotments he grew several sorts, so that he could find out which would be the most productive and make the best wine in England. Over the years he became such an expert that he was consulted by professional vineyard owners. A modest person, he always says of his contribution to British winemaking, 'As an amateur I could try out all these different vines, which I did. Professionals cannot afford to do that; therefore I was able to pass on my findings.'

The great thing about visiting Peter is that just as it is time to leave he will produce a wonderful bottle of wine, and when that is finished, as generous as ever, he will reach for his corkscrew and say, 'I think you should taste this before you leave.'

The digging is shortened by the length of the days, or rather the shortening length of the days. On Saturdays, if the wind is in the right direction, I can hear the roars of the crowd from Queens Park Rangers, for many years the love of my sporting life. Beside me on the ground, as I dig, my radio will be tuned to Radio Five Live, but they are usually ten minutes behind what I already know from the size of the crowd's road that QPR have taken the lead.

I used to train with QPR twice a week and I remember when Dave Thomas, a particularly quick winger, brought in fresh vegetables from his own allotment, and as a result all the other players nicknamed him 'Percy', a throwback to one of the first 'personality' gardeners, Percy Thrower. I cannot imagine any of today's hugely paid players having an allotment!

The next big job is to put up the new metal fencing along most of the site until it reaches the hedge, which in the name of the environment we are keeping. Until now we have had a gradually collapsing chain-link fence that was easy enough to bend down and climb in if you were so inclined. Unfortunately too many people *were* so inclined, especially one regular who apparently used practically to live in one of Mario's sheds. I had never actually come across this person, because he would come at last light and leave at dawn. But there were plenty of clues he left behind, including the fact that he had very big feet, judging by the imprints left on the earth. He didn't steal anything as far as I could make out, although he did once have a spell of damaging winter crops.

We agree to take the fence down section by section, and replace it with the metal fencing which has spikes on the top, and has to be made secure by cementing its posts at every section. Charlie Rycroft and Joe are in charge; in other words they are doing most of the work, although at last there are more volunteers to help them. Tony comes up from the Vale; and one of our new recruits, Dan the archaeologist, does one of the boring jobs of removing spent screws from the bottom of the fencing for the whole length.

The new fence is ugly, in that it cannot be painted the green we would wish, but it will do its job and keep unwanted people out. The work has to be done now when there are no crops to damage or steal, as each night a temporary piece of fencing has to be put where the work will continue the next day. We were given the fencing free by the Park Club in return for putting it up ourselves. It was all part of the agreement that has yet to be signed.

Apart from the work on the fence, this is very much the time of the year for tea and talk and Joe leaves his gas ring on so that the shed is nice and warm when we come in out of the cold. Another Irishman, Steve, a man who has always worked in the open air, is prone to reminisce about his Irish past. He is enthusing about Brunswick cabbage, which he says he only found in Tuckers' catalogue under the heading of Green Manure, which organically keen members grow in the winter and dig in the spring to fertilise their ground naturally. 'I remember a cow back in Ireland,' he says, 'who would not release her milk unless fed Brunswick cabbage at milking time. No

200

cabbage, and she would not drop her milk.'

Joe is taking a rest from the fence. It is a big job, and he makes dry jokes about 'volunteers', or at least the usual suspects who have not volunteered. Michael from the Bromyard site brings laughter when he tells us to note that he had seen Alan Titchmarsh on television, and he said that grass should be turned regularly in the compost bins so that flies do not breed in it. I have flies on the top of one of my bins, where I put the kitchen waste. Yet the compost it has produced would sell in a patisserie, such is its elegance and firmness. We have whole bins of rotting grass, and we find that it melts down and certainly there are no signs of flies. John Johnson has mentioned earlier that Titchmarsh had said you should not put orange and grapefruit skin into the compost bin because it is too acidic. It does not seem to have done my compost any harm. I can only presume TV gardeners' love of decking does not breed flies, but it certainly hasn't contributed anything to the environment.

All forty-five garlic bulbs that I planted in the autumn are now up at least two inches and there are signs of the broad beans I planted in November. The seasons shifting due to global warming? But there has also been quite a bit of heavy rain lately, which delays the digging yet again, and the progress of the fence. So more tea and more chat in Joe's shed.

Evidently it rained so hard at midnight on Saturday that Joe, Michael and others had to delay their departure from The Sun pub in Askew Road!

*　　　*　　　*

Strangely, however, despite dire weather warnings weeks before saying there would be a severe winter it is yet to happen. The more and more machinery these weather people seem to get the worse their forecasts have become. Do they ever pop their head out of doors, or go for a walk, or better still consult an angler?

One December day it is unusually warm, and now all the crops are coming through. Surely danger ahead, because it will only take one frost to halt the broad beans. All the country signs of bad weather ahead are here before our eyes, such as the berries on one of our holly trees which are very red, and have produced a massive crop early on. We need a 'real winter' with frost because that would kill off all the bugs and the white fly that have been allowed to live on by these mild winters. Joe says he has never known a late growing period such as we are experiencing at the moment. I worry about my great parsnip experiment, and long for a good frost, which will help them. In the country they never like to dig their first parsnip until there has been a heavy frost. The trouble is then you would need a road drill to break up the frozen earth to get it out of the ground. The tops look excellent, but when I eventually summon up my courage to dig some for our Sunday evening dinner will there be anything below?

One Saturday afternoon when I'd returned home early I got a phone call from one of the two Scots brothers whose garden backs onto my shed. He says that there is a man cutting a preserved tree on our allotments, and that he should be stopped before he does any more damage. I realise at once that it is John Johnson cutting back the wretched yew tree to give both his and part of my land some more light. There is plenty of tree to be cut without doing any damage. I reply that I will look into it, but there is nothing to worry about, because if it is who I think it is he is just tidying the tree up.

The next day I meet John Johnson and tell him about the call. He is very apologetic, but as we know already he is very skilful with his fuel-driven saw, and amazingly brave at getting up trees on a long ladder and then perching high up as he lops the branches off. The wretched tree will grow again, as it gets strength from pruning.

We often get calls from members of the public, who claim dreadful things are being done by plot holders, usually involving trees. Yet these are the same people who could not have cared less when our whole future was under threat. Or who readily pave over their green piece of front garden so they can park their car, and not have to pay the council for a parking permit. John Johnson is really doing great work with his portable, powerful chainsaw. We have dead trees we want removed near the shop. They are dangerous and in a high wind they could just crash to the ground, because their roots are rotten. They are only a few inches in circumference, not the twelve inches which should not be destroyed. We know that, and don't need interference from ignorant busybody members of the public. I always preach 'come and join us, don't attack us.'

And we have never been so inundated by people who want allotments. In London the lack of allotments has become chronic. This has been caused because people have become much more aware of what they eat, and how it has been affected by chemical spraying, the number of air miles it has travelled, thereby affecting its freshness, and a series of health scares.

As for the number of allotments available, there has been a combination of local authority neglect, and pressure from developers. The Green Party's London leader Darren Johnson, reckons that in some boroughs it would take seven years to get a plot!

Stephen Cole, who took over running Ealing's allotments recently, has spent a lot of his time resuscitating plots on the huge spread of allotments across his borough. But with the Crossrail plan to bring trains across the borough, he is faced with losing at least one whole site. Our own waiting list is lengthy and if some plots do become available it would be a two-year process.

This could become even longer as there has been a huge influx of people into the area, with the development of government offices in Bromyard Avenue into luxury flats. These flat dwellers will not have a garden of their own. A certain percentage of them will no doubt want an allotment. Joe and I have introduced a new hurdle for would-be plot holders to clear. We have been let down too many times by armchair gardeners, as we will politely call the TV garden-show viewers. We are going to ask how the would-be plot holders think they could be of use to the Association. After all, we need bookkeepers, people who will serve in the shop, and various other off-site duties. We just want to get everyone more involved. Therefore, we have been more fortunate with our intake than usual.

One new plot holder is a delightful Muslim mother, whom I remember when my own daughter was below the age of ten and still loved coming to the allotment. We used to wave to each other as she wheeled her own child along Bromyard Avenue. She always seemed so happy. Now she says that she had always looked at the allotments and eventually decided to put her name down for one. At present she does not know too much about the niceties of growing vegetables, but there is plenty of time and support and help around. It is splendid to see someone in Muslim dress working a plot.

As we get more requests for plots, we really need more space, so I have formulated a plan to request the Ealing council to cooperate with us in constructing a community garden scheme in the park, next to Trinity Way, which leads down to two tower blocks of council-owned flats.

The idea is to have a place in front of the gardens for families and children to be able to play and sit down at tables and picnic in safety. Plots would be constructed behind this area. I am told this would be opposed by the head of the parks department, who is very covetous about parks. This park is little used, apart from people walking their dogs, which could easily continue around the site. Parks, like allotments, must change their roles in the future, and not remain blinkered and, literally, rooted in the past.

Joe has already measured out a piece of land, which conveniently is bordered by trees, and, as luck would have it, a permanent official from the council's planning department was looking at something locally. He joined us on the would-be site and thought our plans were quite practicable. Now the round of local politicians must start, and that could take forever. We must not be pessimistic. As we have proved together in the past, anything, and anyone, can be overcome for a good cause. And the meeting at the Mayor's Food For London strategy with a Groundwork representative could be the breakthrough we need. Funding is always available.

I have taken my would-be cookery career a step further by enrolling on the NVQ2 Chef's course at Thames Valley University in Ealing, which means I go there every Monday for four hours, and part of the uniform I have to wear is a chef's jacket with my name embroidered on it. Help! Still, at least I will know what to plant next spring to make the dishes I have learned.

I have planted fifty more cloves of garlic, with Christmas approaching. This is the latest I have ever put it in, but it was as a result of a conversation with a Kent fruit and vegetable grower, Mike Mallett, at Hammersmith farmers' market. He said that he had done it with good results in the past. As he was doing it for a living why should I not do the same thing?

No sooner had I planted this late crop than we had our first real freeze-up of the winter, which inspired Joe to spread the chippings we get from our local Frenchman, who refers to himself on his answerphone as 'the frog'. He is a tree surgeon and delivers us regular supplies of bark chippings. When rotted down they make an excellent additive to the compost bin, but right now we are wheeling the freshly delivered chippings out onto the long path that links the whole site, and have started to spread it at least two inches thick, so that when the thaw comes no one will get their feet muddy.

Joe's eyesight is beginning to worry us. He has suffered for a long time now from fading sight, and at one time there was talk of an operation using lasers, but this has now been abandoned by the hospital. Miraculously it is as if he has memorised the geography of the whole complicated plot. He also knows where everything is in the drawers in his shed, and even more cleverly knows where all his tools are, or should be, in his tool shed. Today I wheel the barrow with chippings and Joe rakes it into place. If I am out on the paths with him I will just talk him along the way, 'go a bit left here Joe,' or 'something in the way on the right.' That is all that is necessary. When he is outside on the pavements he now carries a white stick, for safety.

Back in Joe's shed, Michael arrives from the Bromyard site to help, and says that he has found that by covering his onion sets with the chippings it cuts out all weeds, and has helped them to sprout safely. I decide to do the same thing with my new strawberry bed.

The good thing about barrowing chippings is that after loading each barrowful, which is light work, a fast walk to keep Joe supplied brings out a healthy muck sweat, always good at this time of year.

Christmas approaches, a good time for more than one reason. As far as the allotments are concerned it is because the whole of England seems to take at least a week off, giving plenty of time for the allotment

Although I am nearly always on a diet for coxing an eight on the nearby River Thames, I am getting increasingly interested in cooking after that course at Leith's in the spring. I have always done a bit of the basic stuff, like the Sunday roast, but I have always wondered about making curries and samosas. Now with our new Pakistani member I can learn from an expert. And what with my new course at Thames Valley University, who knows where it will all end?

Another good new member is Charles who was willing to take over another of our 'unlucky' plots, which had been badly tended for the past two years. He is soon digging it back into shape ready to grow something next spring. On Bromyard we have a senior reporter and his wife from the London *Evening Standard*, who is already ferrying barrowloads of chippings and manure down the road to his site, aided by his young son.

We have also introduced half-plots for those who admit they could not handle a full-sized plot, and these are proving very popular. Pattie Christie has taken one of these. She is an elegant lady who works at the Gingko garden centre, which operates from under the arches of an overground part of the tube at the end of Ravenscourt Park. Most of us find its plants, shrubs and trees very nice, but rather expensive. When you are used to growing your own plants from cuttings and seed everything else seems expensive by comparison.

It is a wonderful feeling to observe gardeners who come to us as beginners grow in knowledge and confidence. The BBC girls seem to us to work horrendous shifts, but after a slow start have made superb progress. They have also become involved in the Association, which is even better news. It is this panoply of differing people that makes allotment gardening so interesting.

Fly-tipping is still a danger even in the middle of winter. Our chippings are always supplied by our friendly self-styled 'frog', and no one else. One day Joe and I saw a white lorry drive in. The gates had been left unlocked by one of our members with a car. We saw it at the end of its lightning visit leaving a large pile of chippings and great lumps of wood on the top, as well as hidden beneath. We had been well and truly used by a fly-tipper!

Joe decided then and there to change the lock of the main gate, so that only those with cars had keys. He also had the clever idea of using the small gate made by Adis for the Chestnuts site as a side gate for those on foot. We had never needed it since the new fencing came with a metal gate, so the small well-made gate had been stored at the back of the shop. Now it could be used as a lockable second entrance onto the allotment site.

When people ask about the problems they usually go on about how much of our produce is stolen. I do not like to tempt fate but, the truthful answer is, very little. Several years ago all sorts of things used to go missing, even potatoes. But nowadays we have to thank the supermarket culture for people leaving our home produce alone. Why? Well, supermarkets serve up beautiful-looking vegetables, usually out of season and flown from thousands of miles away; all the same shape and colour, with no mud, already sealed in plastic. So no one likes our mud-covered, oddly shaped produce. Wonderful. The only thing I would ever thank the supermarkets for doing!

In fact, thefts of produce are usually internal, although unless you stay hidden all night, there is no way of proving anything. It is 'local' knowledge. In other words, only someone else on the same plot will know who has what ready, at which time of the year. It will depend if he or she likes that produce and needs it at that moment. Sometimes a 'theft' is purely imagined. We have had several examples of onions being 'taken', but when investigated it is more the forgetfulness of the grower. Or, like an angler describing the size of his catch, the size of a crop can grow in the mind as the grower relaxes in the comfort of an armchair.

In the inner city you can expect vandalism, but hopefully the new fencing will keep the 'weasels' out. 'Hoodies' don't like getting their trainers dirty. So the whole consumer-driven market has guided events in our favour. But, conversely, I am not in favour of locking everything up. If people find things locked they tend to break in, because they think there is something of value to steal.

However, the spread of the car boot sale and online selling has not been good for garden tools, in as far as they vanish more regularly than they used to, no doubt to be sold for a few pounds. One of our members had her cultivator taken. I am afraid in the days we live in, it is not very sensible to keep valuable equipment in a shed. A poor state of affairs, but that is being realistic about life in the inner city. Still, I think things are getting better, if we all act sensibly. If you discover a youngster on your plot do not immediately think the worst and verbally attack him. Ask him how you can help him, whether he wants an allotment. This may all sound very silly, but I actually did this to one youth who then spent an age asking me about planting apple trees, and whether he could do this or that.

Despite the deadness of the time of year, there is still plenty of work to do. I have an old, inefficient and collapsing fruit cage which is a rather grandiose description for something that was first put together for me by the late John Bowtacz. It was excellent when it was finished by John, and contained two or three blackcurrant bushes, a prized redcurrant and a couple of gooseberry bushes, all protected from the birds by netting held up by stout metal poles, and criss-crossed above by light aluminium struts. Now, through continued neglect, it is disintegrating. So first of all I remove the bindweed, whose roots intertwine with those of the fruit bushes. It is like a form of ivy, feeding and finding defence from other plants.

I make the mistake of not wearing gloves. It is always best to wear some sort of hand protection, so that your fingers are not stained like smokers' from the juice that weeds seem to give out. It is never easy to wash away these stains first time, and they can be slightly embarrassing the next day if you have to go somewhere a little more formal than an allotment plot.

Now it is the hidden prongs of the gooseberries that catch me unaware. After all these years I should know better; no wonder gardening books always advise the pruning out of the gooseberry bush from the centre, thus giving easier access to the fruit. It sounds obvious enough. A mere human should have more respect for nature.

There is also the mud to put up with, but my stout leather boots look after that. I'm not so sure I'm doing the ground much good in this mass attack on the undergrowth, but it is about time it was done. At one end there is a huge sapling grown from the seed of a chestnut tree. How quickly it must have taken root and grown. I try sawing bits of it off. I can do the smaller pieces but the main trunk is too thick and difficult to access as I crouch under it in the cage, having my bottom prickled by the gooseberries. Definitely a case for John Johnson and his superb tree saw. However, if it was John's plot it would have been cleared the next day. I am left to wonder why I am a prizewinner in one class that does not appear in flower and veg shows. A prize procrastinator.

My winter digging and sowing of red and white onions remains ahead of time, despite the wetness. One drawback of allotment gardening is that you can only dedicate weekends at this time of year to work on it, because it is dark by tea time. And even at the weekends there will only be a few hours of light. If it rains on that day, you cannot work. There is little else you can do except sit in your shed, shivering, unless you have some form of heat, or drink tea with Joe, which is much more preferable. But the work schedule falls behind through no other fault than that of the weather outside.

The effect of doing the watering for Jerome and Carol while they were on holiday back in the summer is still with me, and I have since spent much time clearing my raspberry bed, and making sure that next year it will look a bit like their orderly rows of canes. I have also cut back the wild blackberry bush, having encouraged it a year ago. My resolution for the new year is to 'Get On Top of Things'. Do it today, not tomorrow. So I have set out how I mean to continue. That watering did me more of a favour than they know!

The wet weather is good for the mid-winter greens that should be eaten soon, although it is the worst year for Brussels sprouts. I am like everyone else who has fine-looking tall green Brussels plants this year, with no sprouts on them at all! Usually I feel our ground is too good and the soil too well fed and soft for growing Brussels, so they don't grow at all or they produce a lot of sprouts, which almost immediately 'blow'. That means they burst open, and no longer have the hard ball you

215

need. Sprouts like to be grown, if possible, in concrete. Hard unfed land is their perfect background for good growth. The trouble with most allotment land is that it has been overcultivated for years, and probably overfed as well. It is far too nice for the ordinary Brussels sprout to flourish.

I still haven't dared to dig my parsnips. Charlie Rycroft grows magnificent parsnips. Long and tapering, thick around the top, just as they look on the seed packets. Of course he rots down huge amounts of grass delivered to him annually, and this compost seems to do the trick. Mine were always weedy little things, about as big as an early carrot. But soon the Great Parsnip Experiment will reveal its results. But I keep putting off the evil day when, no doubt, I will dig them up and find no root at all. Fortunately only I in our family like them, as by the time I have peeled one in the past there has just been about enough to roast two small squares.

This is the time of year when we look after the birds and other animals as the water tanks freeze up. It freezes over Christmas, although there is no snow, so we break the ice on the water in the tanks so that the birds can still lean over and sip the water. We also put some out in bowls on the ground, although this freezes over pretty quickly, and all our old stale bread is broken up and scattered across the frozen earth, because the birds are being deprived of their natural diet of insects. It is amazing how quickly this supply of food disappears, so we have to be sure that we bring them food up every day. No sign now of the cockatoos though. Have they emigrated?

Ever since one of our members collapsed with an epileptic fit, and I was able to call an ambulance on Paola's mobile phone, I always try to remember to bring mine to the allotment. However, it is amazing how many times I have forgotten it. Being out there, often on your own, if an accident happened you could phone home. I feel this especially in John Johnson's case as, bird-like, he perches high up in trees as he lops off first one branch and then another. If he really does go ahead and buy a microlite and start buzzing about the sky above us I don't think he would have time to use his mobile if he got into difficulties.

*   *   *

One day when I am preparing my bean trench for the spring ahead, and digging out the usual bindweed I ducked under the supporting heavy scaffolding pole and it fell on me, hitting me on the back of the head and the side of my hip and leg. It stunned me. I just lay on the ground for a few minutes, and then moved each part of me to see if anything was broken. Everything seemed to function, so I got up rather slowly from a kneeling position. I did not feel too good, and felt for my mobile phone. Needless to say I had not brought it on the very day I needed it! I did some slow stretches, and gradually my body came back to life, although my head still hurt. I was not cut but a lump was developing on part of my head. I felt I should re-enact Basil Fawlty in John Cleese's hilarious *Fawlty Towers* and go back and attack the scaffolding pole that had now crashed completely to the ground. How it had happened I do not know. Tony came over later and showed me that the end had come loose from the fitting that held it; I'd merely had to nudge it for it to collapse on me. Feeling better I then made a bad mistake by retrieving my fork and returning to work. As I reached down to pull out some more bindweed the pain shot up the left side of my body, rather like I imagine an electric shock would be. So that was the end of digging for the day, if not the week. I went back to my own shed, sat down and shelled some runner beans that should have been done long ago, lovely shiny beans falling into the box I had made ready for them.

When I felt a little more settled, but still in pain, I walked slowly but purposefully over to Joe's shed for a reviving mug of tea. He was interested to hear of the incident, and said he would take a look at the fitting to secure it. 'But don't go walking under any scaffold poles,' he joked warningly. The tea was more than welcome.

I decided to loosen up a bit more by going for a long steady walk down the nearby Uxbridge Road to the Lebanese shop, a positive emporium of unusual foods mainly from the Far East, to buy a few things I needed to make a curry.

Most of all I needed a hot soak in the bath with a lot of domestic salt poured into it first. This was a trick I learned when I used to hunt some years ago. After a day in the saddle a few cups of cooking salt thrown into the bath removed all the aches and pains. The large gin and tonic on the side of the bath undoubtedly helped as well! I use this cure, without the gin and tonic these days, after a hard day's digging, and it still works. As, indeed, it worked to free me from the aches and pains this time.

However, I still could not bend down to weed or dig for another three days, and the bruising began to show what a blow I had absorbed, and how lucky I was to get away with it. I have always carried my mobile phone and kept it on whenever I have been on the allotment since that day. At least it taught me something! But Juliet was none too pleased with me, saying that if it had been worse I could have been there all night, and got hypothermia. A bit too dramatic if you ask me!

I look for other things to keep me occupied on the plot while recovering from injury. I see a whole pile of pallets in a front garden on my walk to the allotment. I ask the owner of the house if I could take them and she said 'yes', but that they will be taken away in a few days' time by the builders. Joe and John wheel our flat trolley down to the address the next day in the pouring rain. But they have gone a day early. I feel more of an idiot than ever.

Back in Joe's shed John joins us as we discuss what we are going to grow in the polytunnel in the new season. It had a welcome financial turnover in its first year. I do think we should charge at least 30p a tomato plant this year, because even our customers felt we were undercharging them. It is something when your customers tell you that. Perhaps we could teach the retail trade something after all.

I am now becoming obsessed by polytunnels. They could, for many, be the future. Up in Derbyshire the Welbeck Roads Allotment Trust in Sandiacre got a £2,000 grant from Shell Better Britain and bought a 72-foot-long, 24-foot-wide polytunnel, which they let to twelve plot holders, who control indoor plots 1-foot by 12-foot. There is also a plot run by a primary school. The polytunnel allotment holders say they grow much better crops than they did outdoors.

The way our climate is going polytunnels

must surely play an important part in the future of the allotment movement.

But it would change the view from my shed. And I'm not so sure I would want that, even though at this very moment I am watching a ring dove pecking away at my broccoli! That's the reality, drawback and enjoyment of an allotment.

Winter Recipe

Real horseradish makes a good rib of beef bought at the farmers' market taste even better. Dig up, wash and peel a root of horseradish. It may make your eyes water like chopping onions, but it is very good for a cold! Grate the cleaned horseradish into a bowl, season with salt and butter, and add crème fraiche to taste. You can have it hot or mild.

Your First Allotment

How to get one, and what to do when you get it.

There is definitely a postcode pecking order when you set off in search of your first allotment. If you live outside of a town or city you will probably get hold of a plot quite easily, but if you are within a town or inner city it can be a different matter altogether.

As allotments have regained their popularity—through food scares making people more aware of what they eat and wanting to know where it comes from—so demand has outstripped availability. In some areas the waiting list can mean a wait of several years.

If you want an allotment always contact your local council first, because most of the sites in Britain are council owned. They can also put you in touch with privately owned sites, and generally give you helpful advice. Be forewarned, however, because the attitude held towards allotments by local authorities varies enormously. Some are very keen, as in Birmingham and Bristol, and have full-time allotment officers. Others are not so good, especially in London, where they either provide very few allotments, or seem to have little interest in what is going on with them

223

and do not usually employ a permanent official.

Once you are on a waiting list I would advise an active and positive approach. Keep in touch with allotment association officials and convey to them why you are really keen in getting an allotment, and that is not just a fashionable whim. Also, offer your talents in other directions than just gardening. Every allotment organisation is on the lookout for people who will help in the smooth running of the society. Any skill you can offer will put you ahead of your rivals. In our own association we favour anyone who can offer their services as, for example, an IT expert, or someone who is willing work a two-hour shift in the shop on a Sunday, or who has financial know-how that could lead to them auditing our annual accounts. Knowledge of the law is always useful as well.

Once you have got your plot the hard work begins. Some local authorities clear the land for you. I am against this, as part of the really-wanting-your-own-allotment process is the initial clearing up. Of course, you may take over an already prepared plot, but I doubt it. The reality is that you will have to get used to digging. But first of all take a long look at what you have hired and then go away and draw up a plan. You will never lack advice from your fellow plot holders, so don't be afraid to ask questions.

Your planning should include thoughts about paths as well as what you will grow. Think ahead to wet weather, when you won't want to get your feet muddy just to collect some salad stuff, or in the winter dig some leeks. Keep the things you will want most often near to paths so that you can reach them easily. All this advice might seem obvious, but often when you have taken the wrong decision you will look back and wonder why you did not take the simplest solution. Gardening does not need to be difficult.

First of all you will have to dig your plot, and to do that you will need a good spade. Choose one as you would any piece of equipment that you use regularly. Not too heavy, something that will suit you for years ahead. The same with a fork. Also get a rake and a hoe, and that, for a start, is all you will need. They can be bought quite cheaply at places like B&Q or Homebase, or even car boot sales. But buy quality, do not always go for cheapness. These tools should last you a lifetime. If they are cheap and badly made they will not. Sheffield steel is still the best!

Digging can be a drudge, but it is also an art. Just watch any long-time allotment holder as they dig. They will take it slowly, rhythmically, and will weed as they go. Keep an old bucket beside you as you dig and place all the weeds in it, especially the bindweed that seems rampant on every plot I have ever had. This is a long white root that can go very deep down, so the only way to destroy it is to find where it begins and dig it right out. This can be time consuming, but also very satisfying as your bucket fills with more and more of this pernicious weed. If left, bindweed can strangle any crop you want to grow, as it twines itself, like ivy, around it. Do not be lured by the quick fix of the rotavator, as much as some plot holders may encourage you to use one. The rotavator may be much easier and quicker than digging, but its results are purely cosmetic. It will have cut the wretched bindweed into so many pieces that your plot will be infested with the stuff, as each piece sets about re-growing. In the long run you should compost most of the weeds you pick, except for bindweed, dandelions and anything hard-rooted.

I have referred to digging as an art, and I truly believe that it is. As you finish each session you can look at it and should be able to admire what you have done. Nothing looks better than a well dug patch of earth, neat and level to the last. However, you should not be too keen at the outset, because besides being an art it is also athletic. Just as a marathon runner gradually builds up the distance they run in training, so you must do with your approach to digging. Start with half an hour, and then gradually build to an hour or more if you wish. Remember there is no Olympic medal for digging. Treat it as a pleasure, but it will test the muscles of your lower back and others that you never knew existed before. When you get home it will be worth pouring a cup of household salt into a warm bath and soaking your aches away.

Once you have dug two or three rows along your new plot I advise that you start planting some seeds, or anything else that the season permits. This approach rewards you for the sometimes boring task of having to dig every time you are there. Remember to leave room so that you can continue digging without treading on your newly planted seedbed. Choose something you like to plant. Again, this sounds obvious, but quite often newcomers feel they should grow whatever the rest of us are growing. There are several things to think about here: what costs most in the shops, what you enjoy eating the most, and what you or other members of your family dislike (mine do not share my love of parsnips).

On nearly every British allotment you will see a runner bean frame. But broad beans, which can be planted in the autumn ready for the spring, or in the spring ready for the summer, are far tastier. Eat them young and fresh. Not like those tough old bullet-like versions so many of us were forced to eat for school dinners. Likewise with carrots. When my daughter was younger not many of my carrots reached the kitchen, because they were better eaten raw, straight from the earth and washed under the tap. Even at eighteen she still prefers allotment-grown carrots.

That is the case with many allotment-grown vegetables. They will give you a whole new perception of what vegetables really taste like. I would also recommend the growing of your own shallots and garlic. Both reward you with a lot from a little. You can go down to your local shop and buy two or three garlics, then split them up into cloves and plant each clove, root-side down, six inches apart. Again, there is nothing quite like fresh garlic, with its oily texture that it seems to lose once it has been sent to the supermarket from miles away. By the way, I would not recommend buying Chinese garlic, as in the past I have found it to be most unsatisfactory. Shallots are far better than onions. They taste sharp with a piece of cheddar, or sweeter when finely chopped and used as the basis for a stew or soup. No wonder French chefs always use them, and do not mention the onion. Again, one whole shallot will provide you with at least eight more, each set planted as closely together as the garlic. You can pickle and bottle them quite easily, and for this I recommend using balsamic vinegar. A bit more expensive maybe, but it just gives an extra edge to something you could give as a welcome present. As far as onions are concerned I go for red onions, again grown from what are known as 'sets', like your shallots. These are tiny bulbs you press firmly into the earth, but do not totally bury. You will have to keep an eye on them for the first week, as birds love to mischievously peck them out of the earth. They do not eat them, but it is a game all birds seem to delight in playing. Red onions are milder than the white version, and also look decorative in salads and other dishes.

Allotments are not all about vegetables. When you are settled try some flowers that you can cut and take home, like the wonderful sweet pea, which is so full of scent. You will need a small frame for them to grow up. Easier to grow are statice, which come in many different colours and can either be used as cut flowers in the summer, or dried and hung up through the winter to remind you of the brighter days ahead.

Good luck with starting your own allotment. I hope that you gain as much pleasure from it as I do.